Awakenings

Awakenings

Prophetic Reflections

JOAN D. CHITTISTER

Edited by
Mary Lou Kownacki
and Mary Hembrow Snyder

ORBIS BOOKS
Maryknoll, New York 10545

Founded in 1970, Orbis Books endeavors to publish works that enlighten the mind, nourish the spirit, and challenge the conscience. The publishing arm of the Maryknoll Fathers and Brothers, Orbis seeks to explore the global dimensions of the Christian faith and mission, to invite dialogue with diverse cultures and religious traditions, and to serve the cause of reconciliation and peace. The books published reflect the views of their authors and do not represent the official position of the Maryknoll Society. To learn more about Maryknoll and Orbis Books, please visit our website at www.orbisbooks.com

Manufactured in the United States of America
Manuscript editing and typesetting by Joan Weber Laflamme

Library of Congress Cataloging-in-Publication Data

Names: Chittister, Joan, author. | Kownacki, Mary Lou, editor. | Snyder, Mary Hembrow, editor.
Title: Awakenings : prophetic reflections / Joan Chittister ; edited by Mary Lou Kownacki and Mary Hembrow Snyder.
Description: Maryknoll, NY : Orbis Books, [2021] | Includes bibliographical references. | Summary: "Selected essays by Benedictine Sister Joan Chittister, on themes of women in the church, spirituality, and the Benedictine vision"— Provided by publisher.
Identifiers: LCCN 2021039946 (print) | LCCN 2021039947 (ebook) | ISBN 9781626984646 (trade paperback) | ISBN 9781608339273 (epub)
Subjects: LCSH: Catholic Church—Doctrines. | Women—Religious aspects—Catholic Church. | Benedictines.
Classification: LCC BX1751.3 .C465 2021 (print) | LCC BX1751.3 (ebook) | DDC 230/.2—dc23
LC record available at https://lccn.loc.gov/2021039946
LC ebook record available at https://lccn.loc.gov/2021039947

To Susan Doubet

Contents

Part III
Ever Ancient, Ever New: The Monastic Vision

Acknowledgments

This book is dedicated to Erie Benedictine Sister Susan Doubet. The editors put this book together, but without the generous and painstaking work of Sister Susan, the book would not be published. As Joan Chittister's personal archivist, she made all of Sister Joan's previously published articles readily available, formatted all the content, and solicited all of the permissions from the original publishers. Thank you, Sue, for one more project so masterfully completed.

We would also like to acknowledge Sister Anne Wambach, OSB, for proofreading the text. And, of course, our gratitude to Tom Roberts, the author of Sister Joan's biography, for providing his insightful Foreword. We are also thankful to Robert Ellsberg, editor-in-chief and publisher of Orbis Books, for encouraging this book.

Foreword

Tom Roberts

In the late 1970s, Sister Joan Chittister, then occupying several positions of leadership in the world of women religious, had an opportunity to meet with Cardinal Eduardo Francisco Pironio, prefect of the Vatican office that oversaw religious life. Pironio, known as a champion of human rights in his home country of Argentina, was a man Chittister much admired. She recalls him as a kind man who agreed to meet in his office with her and other women religious leaders. He patiently listened to the case she was presenting.

"Everything that is written about us is written without us," she told him. "The only input that the church takes on the women's issue is what we do on the steps outside your closed doors. After you issue your bulletins defining us as lower and lesser kinds of human beings, we react to them. Dissent is the only ministry a woman has in the church, and when we react you call us radical feminists and heretics."

She said Pironio agreed. "What you say is true," he said. But then he added, "You must only say it here, among us here. You must never say it outside. That is harmful to the church." She said she responded by telling him that women never got

Tom Roberts is former editor of *National Catholic Reporter* and author of *Joan Chittister: Her Journey from Certainty to Faith.*

invited "in here where you decide our lives. We're invisible." She told him, "I will never be quiet. I will not keep that law of silence."

The exchange embodied the debate over women's role in the church that goes on to this day.

The scene in Pironio's office demonstrated that the tension was not so much a product of debate between correct dogma and a violation of tradition. After all, the curial official had told her she was correct. The tension was, and remains, between an undeniable reality—the exclusion of women from positions of real authority and decision-making in the church, including those positions that determined their lives—and a culture intent on maintaining that reality for its own benefit. The texts that follow demonstrate clearly that Chittister kept her promise to the cardinal: she has not been silent.

She has written continuously: books, columns, speeches, essays. She has carried her message around the globe. Well into her eighties, she still sorts through invitations from around the world. She has not been deterred by bishops who have refused to allow her to speak on "Catholic" premises. She speaks in the churches of other denominations, on campuses, at sites where intellectual inquiry and spiritual search go on. She gives retreats, in person and online, and maintains a level of correspondence that would be a full-time calling for most others.

This presentation of her work is, as favor and guide to readers, segmented into major themes. While real life is more complex and interwoven than the page will permit, there is no mistaking in either case that her advocacy for women and their place in church and beyond has been at the core of all she has done from the earliest moments of her public life.

The cause arose initially and remains for her a fundamental issue of justice. The church's treatment of women, is, she believes, not a matter of theological rigor but rather a manifestation of defective anthropology. Perhaps most consequential is her conviction that the church's treatment of women reflects the inadequacy of a God imagined and defined within the tight boundaries of an all-male, celibate, clerical culture.

For Chittister, the issue was never confined to the institutional exclusion of women from ordination. She supports women's efforts in that regard, of course, but it was never central to her work. Her concerns pierce to a much deeper level, to the institution's foundational understanding of God as a male figure, explicable only in male terms. Her questions aim at what she perceives as an institutional flaw that long preceded the ordination rite we know today and that affects all women, not only those who feel a call to formal priesthood.

For challenging such long-held characterizations of God and their implications for women, Chittister was early on tagged a dissenter. It is a label she doesn't dispute. As she told the cardinal, it is a woman's ministry. It is necessary to understand, however, that for Chittister dissent is not synonymous with rupture. Quite the contrary, as she notes in her essay on prophecy. The ancient prophets, she notes, "refused to believe that keeping the rules was the same as keeping the covenant." Religion "was not about the way a people went about ritual," but rather, "about the way people go about life."

Then and now, she announces, "Prophecy lights up the sky with questions."

Her questions rattled the institution, sometimes to the core, and its reactions could be severe. Her agreement to give an opening speech on discipleship at a conference in Ireland dealing with women's ordination brought the wrath of the Vatican down on her and placed her small Benedictine community in Erie in serious jeopardy. The short of it is that the community survived, and Chittister escaped without serious sanction. But the episode demonstrated with a bracing clarity that being a keeper of the kind of questions contained in these pages, questions challenging the institution to take stock of itself and the shaky foundations upon which some central presumptions are constructed, can be a dangerous undertaking.

If Chittister is a dissenter, she is not a contrarian or someone dismissive of tradition. Her fidelity to the Benedictine tradition, one of the oldest in the church, is beyond question. It was a tradition, however, that she began living out, as she puts it, "with one foot in a religious life spawned by the Council of Trent and the other in a religious life awash in Vatican II."

It is understandable, then, that some of the questions lighting up this prophet's little corner of the universe should have to do with the future of religious life in the post–Vatican II world. That question drove her back to Benedict and his sixth-century Rule.

She wrote, "Written in a period of social collapse, of colonial oppression, of ethnic divides, of slavery and classism and patriarchal privilege, on the brink of what historians call AD 536, the worst year ever in the western world, the Rule of Benedict becomes then a model of justice, a beacon of equality, a sign of peace between strangers which we, now, must rekindle in every age."

Chittister has spent a great deal of time plumbing the depths of the Rule and interpreting it for today, investing in the Benedictine way her belief that it contains wisdom enough to save civilization for another fifteen hundred years.

If Benedict—his understanding of the gospel and his model for religious life—is her touchstone, the starting point from which her apologetics on a wide range of issues proceed, Hildegard of Bingen is a soul mate. Chittister writes of Hildegard with an understanding that can only derive from shared passion and familiarity with what it means to dissent, in the Benedictine tradition, as a means of holding an institution to its highest ideals.

Hildegard removed herself and her community of sisters from the oversight of men when such a move was wildly more unthinkable than it is today. She railed against the clericalism of her day and dared to hold the princes of the church in her era accountable for their breaches of trust with the Catholic community. Her refusal to alter her conviction about a matter of justice placed her community in jeopardy. Joan has a soul mate in history. It is not incidental that, nearly a millennium hence, it is Hildegard of Bingen's example and witness and not the actions of those who deemed her out of line that we recall and that the church now celebrates.

Joan's reverence for the founder, Benedict, and such figures as Hildegard of Bingen go a long way in explaining the path of her vocation and her endurance against some significant odds. But it doesn't explain everything.

At the very heart of the matter there has to be more than historic example or an enormous capacity for justice and compassion. That essential, animating force for Chittister is the God of light, the God who cannot be contained, who exists well beyond the limits of our imaginations, a God intimately personal yet beyond our understanding of person.

Benedict is intertwined with her insights into the nature of God, which developed over decades as her growing perception enabled her to free God from the thick carapace of masculine images and characteristics that had accrued over centuries. In Benedict's Rule, she writes, the "first degree of humility, the first step on the way to God, is to have always before our eyes what the ancients call the fear of God—what we know as the sense of God, the awe of God, the awareness of God, the presence of God." Into his era he dared introduce the thought, says Chittister, that our "first step to union with God is knowing that you already have God, you already enjoy God, you already contain within yourself the life that is God."

And if that God is without limit, with dimensions beyond our capacity to understand, then no boundaries exist to contain the prophet's critical gaze, no aspect of life is beyond the curiosity of the spiritual teacher.

The consequence is an offering such as this, a sampling of the prophet's concern as her eye ranges over the civil and ecclesial landscape, calling out the mighty for hypocrisy and injustice, flawed thinking and self-interested authority. And for those seeking the contemplative way amid the "dailiness" of life, the spiritual guide offers wisdom, compassion, and the extended love of a community.

We are all beneficiaries of Joan Chittister's decision early on to take the risk and break the silence.

PART I

WOMEN IN THE CHURCH:
THE FUNDAMENTAL JUSTICE ISSUE

Introduction

The major question facing Christians today is, "What does discipleship mean in a church that does not accept women as full followers of Christ?"

— JOAN CHITTISTER

Sister Joan Chittister wrote this statement in 2000. Women in the Catholic Church are still waiting for the question to be answered. Nonetheless, the institutional church remains, in the second quintile of the twenty-first century, fundamentally patriarchal, hierarchical, and clerical.

And thus, she asks, with the clarion courage of her prophetic voice, "How can the church call the rest of the world to justice, human rights, political participation and equality for all, while at the same time, closing its synods to women, denying its seminaries to women and reserving its sacristies for men alone—muzzling, in other words, one-half of its own population in the name of God?"

Tenaciously, Sister Joan laments the failure of any papacy to affirm the full humanity of women in its administrative structures, liturgical worship and parish ministries, theology, anthropology, and positions of ecclesiastical leadership.

She also challenges images of Mary that fail to affirm her assertiveness, independence, courage and strength, as well as her uncommonly bold faith as a first-century Jewish woman—a truly singular model of female discipleship.

Moreover, in this section Sister Joan highlights the power of female friendship through Janet McKenzie's artistic depiction

"The Visitation" and offers another model of female discipleship as she champions the life of Hildegard of Bingen: "a mystic, a visionary, a reformer—a dissenter."

Poignantly, she urges her readers to develop inclusive images of God by emphasizing the essential place of the Divine Feminine among those images.

Indeed, Sister Joan makes clear that the journey toward fundamental justice for women in the church is unfinished, as is her ongoing call of conversion to mature discipleship. About such matters her prophetic voice will never be silenced.

—MARY HEMBROW SNYDER

1.

Theology of Domination

The notion that women are inferior to men morally and intellectually and must be directed and controlled by them—the theology of domination—is a recurring concept in all the religions of the modern world. The position is, at the same time, contrary to the major tenets of creation held by each of the major religions of the world as well. The resulting subjugation and limitation of the roles of women, however, not only bring into question the integrity of the various teachings of particular religious groups but have implications for the broader social order as well.

The teaching of major religions about women derive primarily from two facets of religious philosophy: one, from the definition of the creative process which serves to explain the origins of human life, and two, from the interpretation of the creation myths of each faith which present models of basic human relationships between the sexes. It is these two concepts which are in tension with one another. The definition of the creative process identifies the manner and substance of creation. The creation myths, on the other hand, describe the roles and functions of the creatures of earth. From these two perspectives come the theological teachings about the nature and purpose of human life. From them also flow the structures, norms and interpretations of human society.

In every major religion the act of creation is described as unitary and equal. The human being is determined to have emanated from a being of pure spirit, a co-equal couple or a hermaphroditic being. In every instance, in other words, creation makes no distinction between males and females. Both males and females, it is taught, have been created from the same substance or same source that is itself without weakness, separation or inferiority. The creative source makes both females and males from the same creative principle.

Based on this point of view, men and women must be equal, capable of like responses, full partners in the human endeavor.

In creation myths, on the other hand, women fall prey to interpretations of blightedness. In the Hindu tradition, Father Heaven must control Mother Earth because she brings forth evil as well as good. Shiva must bring force to bear on Kali to deter her unrestraint from destroying the earth. Buddha's temptation is from the daughters of Mara—Pleasure, Pride and Sensuality. Eve tempts Adam and the human race loses privilege and primal happiness. The fact that Adam is no stronger than Eve in being able to understand or to resist the demonic is ignored in the retelling. The fact that Kali's freedom is forever destroyed without real cause and despite the great good she has done for the human race is overlooked. The fact that Mara's daughters are temptations but not temptresses is given no notice in the analyses. On the contrary, the theological web begins to be spun that women are created by God as carnal or irrational creatures whose role by nature is sexual, whose purpose is secondary, whose value is limited and whose presence is dangerous to the higher functioning of the men of the society. The foundation is laid for women to accept their own oppression as the price of their sanctification. Men, for instance, become the "heads" of the family; women are confined to the home; the way women dress becomes the explanation of why men rape; since women are by nature incapable of more than physical service, public business and "important" matters become the province of men.

The justification for all forms of social diminishment of women is now complete and the theology of domination becomes a tenet of faith. God, who made women equal to men on one level, does not mean for women to have the opportunity to live that equality out in ways open to men. The creation principle and the creation myth become the polar tensions in which women live their lives. The responsibilities they bear on one hand are canceled by the privileges they are denied on the other.

The history of women, as a result, is one of historical and universal oppression, discrimination and violence. In Buddhism, women who have led lives of total spiritual dedication are trained to take orders from the youngest of male monks. In Islam, women are required to veil their heads and cover their bodies to express their unworthiness and signal the fact that they belong to some man. In Hinduism, women are abandoned by their husbands for higher pursuits and larger dowries or held responsible for his death by virtue of a woman's bad karma. In most forms of Judaism, women are denied access to religious ritual and education. In Christianity, until recently and in many sectors yet, the legal rights of women have been equated with those of minor children; wife-beating is protected as a domestic right and even the spiritual life of women is dictated, directed and controlled by the men of the faith.

The theology of domination says, in essence, that men and women are created out of the same substance but that men are superior; that God, in effect, made some humans more human than other humans; that some people are in charge of other people and can do whatever is necessary to maintain that God-given right and responsibility. The social implications of such theology is serious. If God built inequality into the human race, then it is acceptable to argue that some races are unequal to other races. It is clear that the subjugation of whole peoples by another is natural and even desirable. It is obvious that the use of force against other nations and cultures which are considered inferior can be justified and embarked on as a way of life. Even in democracies, some people may be denied the vote because they are inferior, untouchable, unacceptable to those who have gained power, either by force or by natural rights.

The theology of domination makes sexism, racism and militarism of a piece. It brings into clear focus the role of religion in world order, development and peace.

2.

Women in the Church

A New Pentecost in Process

"We used to think that revolutions are the cause of change. Actually, it is the other way around," Erie Hoffer wrote in *The Temper of Our Time*. "Change prepares the ground for revolution."[1] The statement intrigues but it also challenges. If it is true, then little or nothing that characterizes this world at the end of the twentieth century can possibly shape it in the next. Change is everywhere and revolution is sure to follow. Even the Roman Catholic Church, one of whose major teachings is its own inerrant indestructibility, finds itself in the crosscurrents of social revolution so great that only change can possibly, it seems, save it from destruction. The questions that follow from such a perspective, of course, are relatively clear and simple ones: What, if anything, can guide the church through this period of massive change and pending revolution? What will remain of the male-defined church as we know it as new ideas develop? What kind of papacy is needed to deal with the woman's issue in a maelstrom of emerging ideas about women? What does that imply for women? More, what

---

[1] Eric Hoffer, "A Time of Juveniles," in *The Temper of Our Times* (New York: Harper & Row, 1967).

does it imply for the church itself in the next century which, finding itself on the eve of a new millennium, finds itself as well, in the midst of a revolution it would rather not face?

Despite deep differences in the cultural characteristics that enable various societies to accept and adjust to change, rapid and cataclysmic transformation faces the entire world. In villages where the abacus is still being used as the standard system of commerce, the government that shapes the future of the country is fully computerized. In areas where women are in chadors, women's liberation groups lobby publicly to bring pressure to bear on behalf of the legal rights of married women. In regions where machetes are yet the major agricultural tool, black market arms bazaars are putting the world's most sophisticated weaponry in the hands of teenagers. How can that possibly be and what does it have to do with women, let alone the papacy?

In a century that has seen the coming of compulsory education, globalism, space travel, and cloning, change is the ground on which we live, the soil in which we grow, the air we breathe, and the energy that drives our lives. Revolution rides high on the currents of change and revolution is everywhere. Things once considered immutable are as much in flux now as social fads and ocean tides and fleeting time. The tectonic plates of the social world groan with the strain of it. China, for instance, that last mysterious behemoth of the ancient world, is revolting from the isolation of past centuries because of the changes around it. Poor peoples—dislocated, destitute and disregarded across the world—are rising up out of ghettoes and barrios and rain forests in search of political participation and human dignity, because commercial changes, economic and technological changes have made their old world impossible to maintain and the new world inaccessible to them. Death has become an acceptable option for many, no worse than the life they are living now, they say, so whatever the cost to themselves they intend a different world for their children. With the arrival of space travel and the Hubble telescope, the very perception of humanity about itself has been transformed from earth-bound to cosmic.

These are not cosmetic changes. These are not simply minor shifts in the social climate of a world built around a steady-state system. These are not mere cultural adjustments, the kind that come to nations dealing with an influx of immigrants or the internal reorganization of peoples within a given social stratum. The world in which we live now is not simply moving from dynasty to dynasty, from one empire to another empire, from the use of Latin in a church to the prevalence of the vernacular in liturgical practice. No, what is going on around the globe at this millennial moment in time represents a fundamental shift in the human condition. The very perception of life—its character, quality and meaning—changes from biological development to biological development. The size and complexity of the universe both dwarfs and exalts us, magnetizes us and makes us cautious, less sure than ever of what we really know, believe, about the ways of the world. The manner in which society interacts, the notion of differences, and the traditional concepts of human role responsibilities within the group open whole new questions and possibilities for personal development. The self-consciousness of the human race itself, once unabashedly anthropocentric, rests now on the well-being of a fish called the snail darter and the rest of nature as well. This is a step-over moment in the history of the human race, as major surely as the discovery of the New World with its excursion into new modes of governance. It is obviously as paramount as the development of the printing press with its flood of information, and certainly as important as the emergence of the scientific method and the human control of nature that came with it. It is, in fact, a decisive moment in the development of the human race, one that is changing the way we think, the way we see ourselves, the way we relate to others, and the way we deal with institutions. Oscar Wilde in "The Soul of Man under Socialism" put it this way:

> The systems that fail are those that rely on the permanency
> of human nature, and not on its growth and development.
> The error of Louis XIV was that he thought human nature
> would always be the same. The result of his error was the
> French Revolution. It was an admirable result.[2]

Changes change things, regardless of social resistance. A whole
generation of people do not like computers, for instance, but
computers have already changed the way we work, the way we
think, and the way we relate to one another. What we like or
do not like, in other words, cannot arrest the effects of what we
know. Change is not coming; change is here.

No institution need consider itself spared in the process—not
the state, not the economic system, and certainly not the church,
whose theology is daily challenged by changing concepts of creation, of life and of human nature itself. Nevertheless, the struggle
of traditional institutions to maintain the past in the face of a
frightening future has seldom been clearer in all of history if for no
other reason than because it has seldom been so global. Change is
not now simply a national incident, it is an international upheaval
the proportions of which are only recently beginning to come
into focus. Eruptions in the state, schisms in the churches, demonstrations in the streets of the world all attest to the rise and swell of
a new consciousness which old systems are neither prepared, nor
willing, to accommodate. Corporations duck and feint, and hide
and run from the workers of the world to produce the greatest
number of goods for the least amount of investment. Fueled by
profit rather than justice, their loyalties know no national boundaries. Only now are the poor of the world beginning to realize that
their problems do not lie with the poor workers of other countries. Their problems lie with the wealthy corporations of their

---

[2] Oscar Wilde, "The Soul of Man under Socialism," *Fortnightly Review*
[London] (February 1891; repr., 1895).

own countries who move plants and products at will in order to avoid worker compensation laws everywhere. Governments, too, restrain the citizens of the world by want, force, collusion, or lies in order to maintain power that is often bought and always sold to the highest bidder. Religion itself clings to forms that sacralize the system, controlled by priestly castes, rather than to the values within it that could make change a holy and empowering experience for everyone, not simply women. Through it all, men—and men only, in large part—make the decisions, determine the directions, and decide the operations that decide the fate of the rest of the world—plant, animal, mineral, and woman.

Christianity, perhaps, finds itself in a particularly grave situation in the face of changing expectations, understandings and insights. To preach a God of love who, on the one hand, created women and men out of an identical substance, and a God of power, on the other, whose machoism has supposedly put one gender under the control of the other; to define God as all Spirit, on the one hand, and as exclusively male on the other; to proclaim a God who makes both men and women in the divine image, but then defines one part of that humanity as less human than the other; to profess a God who calls us all to a knowledge of salvation but gives men alone the right to designate exactly what that means: this implies, requires, posits a God who is very inconsistent indeed. It is a theological problem of mammoth proportions. And in a world where women, too, get PhDs in theology and philosophy, in science and in history, past answers do not persuade. The woman question is not going to go away no matter how clearly the church says it must. Male hegemony of human thought has had its day. There is another voice to be heard now, rich in experience, full of questions, and very other in its values, goals and perceptions than those touted by a male church throughout a first millennium.

Women are intent on bringing their own piece of the wisdom not only to the development of the human race but to the reinterpretation of a faith that once taught racism, anti-Semitism and slavery with as much confidence as it does sexism in our day. The question, of course, is: How can a church that applies one set of principles to the public arena fail to apply the same set of principles to itself? How can the church call the rest of the world to justice, human rights, political participation and equality for all, while at the same time closing its synods to women, denying its seminaries to women and reserving its sacristies for men alone—muzzling, in other words, one-half of its own population in the name of God? How can "tradition" possibly be an answer in a church where tradition in every other category is simply the interpretation of the time? This pope, for instance, had no trouble in asserting the equality of women in *Mulieris dignitatem*, despite the church's unbroken theological tradition that had labeled them naturally inferior for centuries.

Fundamentalists, of course, want to call feminist theology, feminist philosophy, and feminist participation in the process of church, heresy. A multitude of historical parallels arise to lend editorial comment and bring discrimination to the discussion. There have been, as a matter of fact, a number of things the church once called "heresy" and punished heretics for believing that have then become the theological coin of the realm. Scripture study, for instance, was once considered heresy. It was called "private interpretation" and in defiance of the accepted exegesis of the church.[3] Support for the pluralistic state was called heresy.[4] To believe in the separation of church and state in the face of a theocratic tradition was called modernism and a sin against faith. Acceptance of what Vatican II later termed "whatever else is true" in non-Christian re-

---

[3] Wolfgang Bienert and Francis Schussler Fiorenza, eds., *Handbook of Catholic Theology* (New York: Crossroad, 1995), 650–652; also Raymond Collins, "Scripture, Interpretation of," in *Encyclopedia of Catholicism* (San Francisco: HarperCollins, 1995), 1173–1175.

[4] Bryan Hehir, "Church and State," in *Encyclopedia of Catholicism,* 314–317.

ligions was, without reserve, considered heresy. Even participation in the worship services of other Christian churches was considered sinful.[5] Let the thoughtful beware. Such historical perspective taxes a person's patience with decrees designed to deter discussion of one of the most important issues of the time. How Christian is it to agree to say nothing in the face of the primacy of conscience when the greatest moral issues of the moment challenge both the theology and the practice of the church? And if the question of women can be routinely struck from the agenda of the church by papal fiat, then why not nuclearism, why not genocide, why not abortion—all of which, among others, deal in one way or another with questions of creation, life and power? In fact, why not strike anything that a pope considers dangerous to the historical grist of the church?

The fact is that two-thirds of the poor of the world are women, two-thirds of the illiterate of the world are women and two-thirds of the hungry of the world are women. There has to be a reason for that. Oppression of half the human race cannot be explained as an accident. Oppression is a plan. Oppression is a philosophical position. Oppression is a theological posture, a theological schema, a theological concept made holy because some have said it is so.

The church that purports to witness to the living presence of Christ in time finds itself in a papacy functioning in the present but, where women are concerned, at least, embedded in the philosophy, theology and anthropology of the past. The fact is that the status of women has changed, at very least in the mind of women themselves if not completely yet in the structures of the society around them. The church shall not be spared the revolution that comes from that kind of axiomatic change in self-perception.

---

[5] Stanislaus Woywood and Callistus Smith, *Practical Commentary on the Code of Canon Law* (New York: Joseph F. Wagner, 1952), 513.

"Woman," it seems, is an admissible subject for reflection, discussion and development everywhere but in the church as we know it in the twentieth century. And yet, within its very self, the church as we know it harbors the seed of equality that makes the revolution imperative. At the same time, the church, it seems, is the last institution to honor it.

The papacy that fails to deal with so fundamental a change in the perceptions of humankind will be the papacy that presides over the philosophical demise of the church. Whether or not the church can possibly last without women is an important but debatable question. After all, male clubs and sanctuaries have time-honored histories and may surely survive as some kind of male bonding experience or elite fraternity. Whether or not the church can possibly live, whole and entire, authentic and true, without women, is not debatable at all. The very suggestion of such a thing flies in the face of the Jesus-story itself.

The scientific revolution, once the very bastion of the male control of nature, has in our own lifetime put the lie to male autonomy—to any autonomy at all as a matter of fact—and to the notion that the world was made for the disposal of man, identified always as "male" unless specifically noted otherwise by canons and customs and papal decrees.[6] But with the simple scientific awareness that life is not a ladder but a weave of differences went male pre-eminence and human primacy as well. Suddenly, the story of creation drew another look and newly rediscovered theological theses with it.

Theological Theses

The Genesis 1 story of creation with its emphasis on man as the crown of creation and creation as a kind of cornucopia filled

---

[6] John B. Cobb, Jr., "Ecology, Science and Religion: Toward a Postmodern Worldview," in Mary Heather MacKinnon and Moni McIntyre, eds., *Readings in Ecology and Feminist Theology* (Kansas City: Sheed & Ward, 1995), 236–238.

with the rest of nature for the sake of human satisfaction became the paradigm of Judeo-Christian thought.[7] Its theme was human transcendence; its thesis was domination. Forgotten, unfortunately, was the correspondingly determinative message that God saw all creation as equally "good," that the Sabbath—reflection, contemplation, harmony—not man, was the crown of creation. Gone, too, were the sobering insights of Genesis 2, as well, that God brings the animals to the human to name, not to give him the right to destroy them but to require him to understand the depth of the relationship between humanity and those for whom humanity had a personal responsibility. The message is subtle but effective: The rest of creation has no need for humanity, but humanity cannot exist at all without the rest of creation. The theme of Genesis 2 was companionship; its thesis was human dependence on the rest of creation.

Humanity, and the church, as well, built its institutions on Genesis 1. Hierarchy was a given. All things were in the service of men. Males were made in the image of God. Women were made from man. Women were "natural" by virtue of a physiology designed for birthing rather than thinking.[8] Men, on the other hand, whose bodies were not suited for anything inherently creative, must then obviously be suited for the things of the soul; the things of the mind, of course; and the spiritual things of life, obviously. Man/the male was, therefore, closest to God, the theologians argued, because it is the mind that reflects the essential attribute of God—the spirit. In the hierarchy of creation, in other words, instead of gaining because they have both creative body and rational soul, women are defined by their bodies and robbed of the quality of their souls. So spoke all the great theologians of

---

[7] Michael J. Himes and Kenneth R. Himes, "The Sacrament of Creation: Toward an Environmental Theology," in Mary Heather MacKinnon and Moni McIntyre, eds., *Readings in Ecology and Feminist Theology* (Kansas City: Sheed & Ward, 1995), 272–274.

[8] Joan Chittister, OSB, *Heart of Flesh: A Feminist Spirituality for Women and Men* (Grand Rapids: Eerdmans, 1997), 32.

the church—Augustine, Origen, Thomas Aquinas and every lesser light after them. "Not in the body but in the mind," Augustine wrote, "was man made in the image of God."[9] Woman ("derived" they argued, rather than formed from the same material—"Bone of my bone, flesh of my flesh") was made, not in the image of God but in the image of man. So spoke them all. So speak them still.

The thought process is plain: God is utterly other—the ultimate. And so matter, nature, is without value. Nature loses. And woman loses, too.

Francis Bacon's explanation of his scientific method articulated the theology clearly. "Man fell," Bacon explained, "and lost dominion and can regain dominion through scientific study."[10] Dominion, a male prerogative, became the Holy Grail of a science that had flowered in the service of theology. Then Bacon concluded, "Nature is to be bound into service like a slave."[11] The stage is set. Everything is now in place. What theology asserted, science confirmed. Darwin's survival of the fittest fell on ready ears. The Industrial Revolution, colonialism, and "development" became its necessary and dangerous corollaries. Sexism was its given. The world, after all, had been made for humanity, for us, true, but, note well, for the fittest of it. And men, the theologians said, the scientists confirmed, and the philosophers argued, were the fittest of all. Woman is, symbol-using, yes, but inferior, intermediate, for purely instrumental purposes. A

---

[9] Augustine, *Commentary on the Gospel of John XXIII* 10, as quoted in Grace M. Jansen, "Healing Our Brokenness: The Spirit and Creation," in Mary Heather MacKinnon and Moni McIntyre, eds., *Readings in Ecology and Feminist Theology* (Kansas City: Sheed & Ward, 1995), 285.

[10] Francis Bacon, *Novum Organum* (*Works,* Part 2, Vol. 4, p. 247), as cited in Carolyn Merchant, "Feminists Perspectives on Science," in Mary Heather MacKinnon and Moni McIntyre, eds., *Readings in Ecology and Feminist Theology* (Kansas City: Sheed & Ward, 1995), 338–341.

[11] Francis Bacon, *The Great Instauration,* written 1620 (*Works,* Vol. 4, p. 20), as quoted in Carolyn Merchant, *The Death of Nature: Women, Ecology and the Scientific Revolution* (San Francisco: HarperCollins, 1983), 169.

glorified potted plant. And they said so, these fine philosophers, these holy theologians—all of them. Over and over again.

Philosophical Theses

Jean-Jacques Rousseau said a woman could be educated—but not for herself, and not even for the good of society, but only for the advancement of her husband.[12]

John Stuart Mill said a woman could be educated, yes, but only in order to preserve society by being fit to maintain the social standards set by men. An ill-educated wife, he argued, would lead to the deterioration of society.[13]

In 1969, Claude Levi-Strauss said a woman could be educated in order to maintain the domestic system on which men depend to control the public one.[14]

And Pope John Paul II, philosopher, said again in the 1990s that women had "special nature" for "a special purpose." To maintain the home, apparently, but not the theology of the church.[15]

The patriarchal worldview that follows from those premises is a clear one: It is hierarchical in structure, dominative in essence, dualistic in evaluations and male in its norms. It rests on the premise that some of us were made to be—are meant to be—better than the rest of us, that some of us are in charge of the human race and we know who we are. It is, in other words, a recipe for conflict, struggle, sexism, racism, suppression, oppression and revolution. And we are in it. And it is everywhere. And it has come to white heat in our day, in our time, in this century.

---

[12] Moira Galens, *Feminism and Philosophy: Perspectives on Difference and Equality* (Bloomington: Indiana University Press, 1991), 17.

[13] Ibid., 30.

[14] See Claude Levi-Strauss's argument in *The Elementary Structures of Kinship* (Boston: Beacon Press, 1969).

[15] Pope John Paul II, *Mulieris dignitatem*, August 15, 1988, in *The Pope Speaks* 34 (1989): 10–47.

Structural Implications

The results of a thought process based on domination is a clear one. The dualism that defines women as "natural" rather than spiritual and nature as inferior in the face of the all-spiritual God makes a clear distinction between the social roles of women and men. Women are born for childbearing, "mothering" is their lifetime task and serving the needs of men is—like the rest of nature—their primary function. Men, men said, exist to dominate the realm of ideas, to determine the operations of life, and to enjoy the fruits of nature. For them, fathering is an event. Echoes of these ideas ring in every debate of its kind to this day. Institutions are shaped by them. The church encourages them. The Jesus whose ministry was supported by women, spread by women, announced by women and shared by women finds little to recognize in the designs of nature here.

Women, not made of sacred substance, the arguments imply, have no part of sacred things in a cosmogony such as this. Woman's domain is domestic. Woman's legal rights are limited. Women need men, literally, to be their "heads." The capstone to the argument is a simple one: God did it this way and so, clearly, God wants it this way. Try as they might, there is nothing men can do about the matter to situate women in the same human position as men. As if they were not, in the first place, themselves responsible for an interpretation of scripture that makes it so.

Throughout the world to this day, men control the public sphere and all the laws that the public sphere develops to control both nature and women. Since men, the males of the species, are normative they know what is good for everyone and everything else. The conundrum, of course, is that science has betrayed the triumvirate of philosophy, theology and anthropology. We know that men are mightily natural and women are clearly rational. We know now that we can't have it both ways. Either women are different and must, therefore, be heard from out of their own experience, as subjects, not objects, as moral agents, not as moral minors. Or women have the same human, moral and intellectual acumen as men and, therefore, hearing from them is to be taken for granted. As it is, the gifts of women are, for the most part, being lost to society as a whole, and to the church, in particular, where the spirituality of women has long been the backbone of the faith but ignored at every level.

But with the pillars of hierarchical thinking weakened on every side, there is no justification for the suppression of peoples and no way to sustain it other than through brute force. Change has begun the revolution.

The confinement of women as a class to the domestic dimensions of society rings false.

A New Papacy for Women

The problem for women in a church in the midst of change is that they live with a papacy that theoretically belongs to the last century, canonically governs in the present, and provides for the future out of an anthropology now defunct. Both science and philosophy have now denied the kind of hierarchical, dualistic definitions of life that have sustained domination throughout the first millennium. What we need now is theological leadership that will do the same. We need a papacy that can see the oppression of women by the church itself and is willing to model their inclusion at the highest levels of the Vatican planning itself. The implications of that for the church, however, are major. Words alone will not do it. The next papacy will be required to demonstrate a clear acceptance of the equality of women or the credibility of the church in a world awakening to equality all the way from the Little League baseball teams of the western world to the parliaments of world governments, will be severely, if not mortally, compromised. The notion that God does not want for the church what God apparently wants everywhere else in humankind strikes a specious chord on the human ear. The implications are clear:

The Theological Insights of Women Must Be Recognized. For two thousand years the thinking of the church has been almost exclusively male. Little or nothing of women's experience, interpretation and insights have been incorporated into official church documents. The truth of the matter is that the Catholic Church operates as if women are not in it. The effect on women has been negative, of course, but the effect on the church has been worse. Under no condition can it claim to have seen the Lord with two eyes.

If women are really reasonable creatures, however, then they are theology-thinking human beings. That theologizing must be fostered, recognized, heard. The next papacy must name women to all theological commissions, encourage their presence on seminary faculties around the world, seek their interpretations and listen intently not only to their emerging questions but to their answers to theological issues, as well. When early theologians—Clement, Origen, Augustine, Anselm, John Climacus and a multitude of others—engaged in heated exchange over issues basic to the faith, the process met with respect. The church weighed each position thoughtfully and seriously. Now, women must be included in that same theological debate with that same sincerity, or the work of the church is only half finished.

To design the doctrines of the church on salvation, sexuality, marriage, family, and sin—all of which affect the lives of women equally but differently than they do the lives of men—without formative input from women themselves conveys positions that are incomplete as well as arrogant. The continuing questions of women over time have pointed out the fault lines of the faith; the theological answers of women to the theological questions of the age may demonstrate both its partisanship and its plausibility, as well. Until then, the answers of male theologians to women's questions will remain forever suspect. When the Canaanite Woman challenged the justice and theology of Jesus toward outsiders, it was a process of conversion that took place—both his and hers—not authoritarianism, not oppression.

The question "What do the scriptures say to women?" needs to become a part of every course, a concern in every document, a clue to deeper meanings and a guide to more meaningful insights for the church at large if scripture is ever to reveal itself to the whole Christian community. Scripture study that excludes women at the highest levels of discourse is study that hears, sees, and feels only one-half of the message in the material. The leadership of Miriam, the autonomy of Mary, the commissioning of the Samaritan Woman, the teaching of Martha have for far too long been ignored or, at best, only superficially accounted for by standard male exegeses. Tomes have been written, for instance, on the stoning of Stephen or the identity of the unnamed young man in the Garden of Gethsemane, but hardly a word on the saving of Moses by two women, two enemies, two subverters of the system they both rejected, one the slave, the other the princess. A great deal has been inferred about the priests of Baal, almost nothing about the Jewish midwives, Shiphrah and Puah. It is time to see the women in scripture as much the messengers of God, the leaders of the people, the saviors of the faith, as the men were.

The Spiritual Insights of Women Must Be Made Available to the Entire Church. The church needs women as spiritual directors. The papacy of the next millennium must take special care to include the spiritual insights of women in the direction of the church. Feminist spirituality is as essential for men as it is for women because it develops an entirely new worldview, in contradiction of the values spawned by patriarchy and institutionalized in the church. Feeling, compassion, inclusiveness, community and globalism, among others, must begin to bring balance to the kind of cold rationality, individualistic asceticism, elitism, authoritarianism and autonomy that have characterized spirituality in the past.

Women spiritual directors must certainly become part of every seminary program, every chancery office, every spirituality course taught, and every diocesan retreat given. Priests especially must have the opportunity for women spiritual directors if, for no other reason, than to develop their own sensitivities to the point where they can minister to women at large comprehendingly and respectfully. To be in a church where official Vatican directives deny a seminarian the right to have a mature woman as a spiritual guide is a very clear signal that the men of the church have nothing whatsoever to learn about the faith from the women of the church. It is a clear message, and a false one. The question that follows it for women is, "Why stay?"

The Ecclesiastical Leadership of Women Must Be Institutionalized. The Roman Catholic Church, universal in definition, human in scope, has no right to be either a male or a clerical preserve. The church is not male. It simply looks that way. In order to develop a real Christian community—one that thinks and acts and witnesses together—the synods of the church must include women, the curial congregations of the church must be headed by women, the cardinalates of the church, until 1917 granted to laity as well as to clerics—Giovanni de Medici in the fifteenth century and Giacomo Antonelli in the nineteenth, for instance[16]—must also be opened to women, as well. Diocesan offices and parishes must be routinely pastored by dedicated women whose commitment to living the gospel by participating fully in the church is not hindered by the church itself. The next papacy, to be credible in a changing world, will need to demonstrate within itself what will soon be common coin around the world—the human community in tandem, learning from one

---

[16] *Encyclopaedia Britannica*, 15th ed., "Leo X" (Giovanni de Medici), vol. 7, 274–275; and "Giacomo Antonelli," vol. 1, 465–466.

another, supporting one another, respecting one another, loving one another to fullness of life.

The Ordination Question Must Be Allowed the Impulse of the Spirit. To deny the church as a whole the right to discuss the issue of either women deaconesses, women priests or a married clergy speaks of the flimsiness of the theological positions which underlie their canonical definitions at the present time. To risk the loss of the sacraments in a sacramental church by preferring maleness to priesthood is a breach of faith even more serious, perhaps, than simple authoritarian administration. Finally, to confuse the Jesus of history with the Christ of faith and to deny half the human race the right also to "remember Him" when they gather makes for very profound theological concerns.

Respected theologians everywhere admit the validity of the questions. The question of the ordination of women is far more than a woman's question. Protestant Christianity, prophet to the Roman Catholic Church for centuries by virtue of its preservation of scripture study, may well now be required to preserve the Eucharist as well unless something is done to free it from its male confines. Clearly, the church in the next millennium needs a papacy willing to trust the movement of the Spirit on these issues before the Christian community dissolves into a collection of distant individuals and Eucharist itself becomes, at best, only a pallid memory of a faith once vital but now defunct.

"A living thing is distinguished from a dead thing," Herbert Spencer wrote in his 1895 landmark volume, *Principles of Biology,* "by the multiplicity of the changes at any moment taking place in it."[17] We are dangerously past due some important changes, perhaps, if we want to do more than exist as a church. The papacy that does not deal with the spiritual imperative of the ordination of women may well be presiding over a dead church.

---

[17] Herbert Spencer, *Principles of Biology,* part 1, chap. 4 (1864).

The next papacy will not simply be held accountable for the male administration of a male church. The next papacy will be accountable, where women are concerned, with breathing some life into it.

The Question of the Nature of God Must Be Revisited and Publicly Reshaped. If women are to find themselves in the church, they must be able to find themselves in the Godhead, as well. God-language that requires the all-spiritual God to be "father" and denies the womb and breasts of God of which Isaiah speaks also smacks of the heretical itself. The church that is willing to call God a hundred names—rock, key, door, root, hen and tree—but never, ever "mother" needs a thorough examination of conscience. There must be a reason to skew, contradict, and contort the obvious with such vehemence. It is time to determine, to face, and to repent the kind of sexism that fears even the feminine in God. There must be something in the male psyche of church that insists on projecting onto the female its fears of itself. God-language itself unmasks the fragmentation in the church's understanding of God. It is time for the church to become whole. It is time for the papacy to lead us out of such a tangled theological morass, back to the Jesus of lepers and outcasts and women, of beseeching women and proclaiming women and ministering women, of women with reckless faith, and fearless presence and interminable fidelity.

We need a Pentecost papacy in the next millennium that can hear the many voices of women—each speaking in her own tongue—and understand them.

The time is short. After all, as Eric Hoffer taught us, "We used to think that revolutions are the cause of change. Actually, it is the other way around. Change prepares the ground for revolution." And change is here—whether the papacy is or not.

3.

Discipleship

The Questionable Measure of Christianity

The poet Basho writes: "I do not seek to follow in the footsteps of those of old. I seek the things they sought." It is a lesson in discipleship that we may all need to learn again if the church itself—from papacy to people—is to be counted among the disciples of Christ.

Today, as seldom before, the church, both as institution and as the people of God, is being forced to choose between imitation and discipleship. To confuse one with the other is to skew the whole Christian enterprise. The only really meaningful question for a Christian is how to make Jesus relevant, real today. At one level, that can't be done. The Jesus of history does not live in our time. At another level, if Christianity is to have any meaning at all, making Jesus relevant now must be done. What Jesus came to be, to do, to create must be made real in us today or Christianity does not live at all. But to do that it is necessary to consider first, what the notion of discipleship really implies and secondly, what the call to discipleship demands now. The two dimensions are inextricably linked: what discipleship implies is clearly what it demands. The concept and the call are of a piece.

If not, discipleship becomes either play-acting or faddism. In the first case we will take discipleship to mean that we must do only what Jesus did—as if we could. In the second case, we will do only what we feel like doing—as if we should—and say we do it because of Jesus.

One of the major questions facing the institutional church today is the place of women in the life of the Christian community. Some people argue that in answering the question of the time, we can only do what Jesus did. Others maintain that we can't minister in this world at all unless we seek what Jesus sought—equality, justice and all-inclusive love. The issue hinges, I think, on the theology of discipleship that energizes the people of God: priests, people and popes together.

The facts speak for themselves. Christian discipleship is a very dangerous thing. It has put every person who ever accepted it at risk. It made every follower who ever took it seriously on alert for rejection, from Martin of Tours to Dorothy Day, from the early church to the present time. It cast every fragile new Christian community in tension with the times in which it grew from then to now.

To early Christian communities it meant to defy Rome, to stretch Judaism, to counter pagan values with Christian ones. It demanded very concrete presence; it took great courage, unending fortitude and clear public posture. It took the rejection of emperor worship, the foreswearing of animal sacrifice, the inclusion of gentiles, the supplanting of dependence on the Law with a commitment to love recklessly. And all. And everyone.

The following of Christ was not an excursion into the intellectual, the philosophical, the airy-fairy. It was real and immediate and cosmic. "Come, follow me," became an invitation to defend the poor, an obligation to peacemaking in warring societies, a call to identify with the outcasts of society, an experience of public disapproval and personal exclusion. Discipleship became the step-over point between philosophy and sanctity.

The problem with Christian discipleship is that instead of simply requiring a kind of academic exercise or personal piety—the conventional understanding of most kinds of "discipleship," religious or otherwise—Christian discipleship qualifies as authentic only when it demonstrates publicly what it claims to hold on a personal level. Christian discipleship requires a kind of living that is sure then, eventually, to tumble a person from the banquet tables of prestigious boards and the reviewing stands of presidents and the parliaments of empires to the most suspect margins of society. Because the disciple of Christ looks for a new world order based on right relationships, on justice and on love—on a Jesus-perspective—in a world that builds social relationships on personal gain, personal life on acquisition and the civic order on charity without social change, discipleship invites tension. To follow Jesus, in other words, is to follow the One who turns the world upside down.

It is a tipsy arrangement at the very least. People with high need for approval, social status and public respectability need not apply. "Following Jesus" leads always and everywhere to places where a person would not go, to moments of integrity we would so much rather do without. It is not doing what Jesus did; it is seeking what Jesus sought.

The Christian, then, carries a worldview that cries for fulfillment now. Christian discipleship is not preparation for the hereafter. It is the commitment to live now as if the Reign of God had already come—so that it may. To follow Christ is to set about fashioning a world where the standards into which we have been formed may well become the standards we find that we must ultimately foreswear. Flag and fatherland, profit and power, chauvinism and sexism done in the name of Christ are not Christian virtues whatever the system that looks to them for legitimacy. To follow Christ is to honor all creation, not simply the country in which we are born; to profit the other, not simply the self; to cross boundaries and recognize all of humanity as valid and valuable. Christian discipleship is not about doing what Jesus did. It is about living in this world the way that Christ lived in his.

It is a very demanding process. Discipleship implies now, just as it did then, a commitment to leave nets and homes, positions and personal security to be now in our own world what Christ was for his—healer and prophet, voice and heart, call and sign of the God whose design for this world is justice and love, who hears the poor Lazarus and ministers to the abandoned Hagar. Christianity at its best confronts a world bent only on its own ends with a picture of what a new world based on the heart of Christ would look like, whatever the cost. The price is a high one. Discipleship cost Martin of Tours his status, Dorothy Day her reputation, and Martin Luther King his life.

The problem is clear: to claim discipleship, the church must not only preach the gospel, it must model it. And surely it must never obstruct it. Religion that colludes with the dispossession of the poor in the name of patriotism becomes just one more instrument of the state. Religion that blesses oppressive governments in the name of obedience to authority makes itself an oppressor as well. Religion that goes mute in the face of massive militarization practiced in the name of national defense abandons the commitment to the God of Love for the preservation of the civil religion. Religion that condones the pauperization of women in the name of motherhood and denies the ministry of women in the name of God's will flies in the face of the Jesus who overturned tables in the Temple, contended with Pilate in the palace, chastised Peter to put away his sword and, despite the theological teachings of the day, commissioned women to preach his name and raised a socially useless girl-child from the dead.

Clearly, discipleship is not based on civil quietism and private piety. Still less is it based on preaching one thing and institutionalizing another. On the contrary. Discipleship confounds right reason and good sense with right relationships and good heart.

It pits the holy against the human. It pits the heart of Christ against the heartlessness of an eminently sensible world. To be a disciple is to find ourselves in contradiction. We become purveyors of a world where the weak confound the strong. We come to proclaim that humility raises a person up and pride destroys. We begin to seek a world where the rich and the poor change places. We set out to shape a world where the last are made first. We insist on a world where women have the right to do what heretofore has been acceptable only for men because they are humans, because they, too, have been called to discipleship. The Reign of God becomes a foreign land made home. "Come follow me" becomes an anthem of public proclamation and human liberation.

Discipleship, we know from the life of the Christ whom we follow, is not membership in a social club called a church. Discipleship is not an intellectual exercise of assent to a body of doctrine. Discipleship is an attitude of mind, a quality of soul, a way of living that is not political but which has serious political implications, that changes things because it simply cannot ignore things as they are, things that defy the will of God for humanity.

The disciple takes public issue with the values of a world that advantages only those who do not need to be advantaged, takes aim at institutions that call themselves freeing but which keep half the people of the world in bondage, takes umbrage at systems that are more bent on keeping improper people out of them than they are in welcoming all people into them, takes the side always of the poor despite the power of the rich. Discipleship cuts a reckless path through corporation-types like Herod, institution-types like the Pharisees, system-types like the moneychangers and chauvinist-types like apostles who want to send the women away.

Discipleship stands bare naked in the middle of the world's marketplace and, in the name of Jesus, cries aloud all the cries of the world until someone, somewhere hears and responds to the poorest of the poor, the lowest of the low, the most outcast of the rejected. Anything else, the gospels attest, is certainly mediocre and surely bogus discipleship. Christianity is human community writ large and discipleship is its voice.

It is one thing, then, for an individual to summon the courage it takes to stand alone in the eye of a storm called "the real world." It is another thing entirely to see the church itself be anything less than the living Christ. If the church is to be relevant, if the church is to be a community of disciples, then it must be inclusive. To see a church of Christ deny the poor and the outcast their due, justify the very systems in itself that it despises in society, is to see no church at all. It is at best religion reduced to one more social institution designed to comfort the comfortable but not to challenge the manacles that bind humanity to the cross. In this kind of church, the gospel has been long reduced to the catechism. In this kind of church, prophecy dies and justice whimpers and the truth becomes too dim for the searching to see.

The church stands at the crossroads of discipleship today, choosing between community and club, between the prophetic and the institutional, between the gospel and a law designed to cut half the world out of their spiritual birthright if baptism is really baptism at all.

Today, as never before in history, perhaps, the world and therefore the church within it, is being stretched to the breaking point by life situations that, if for no other reason than their immensity are shaking the globe to its foundations. New life questions are emerging with startling impact and relentless urgency. The poor are crying for humanity. The outcasts are demanding a seat at the tables of the world. The living dead are wailing resurrection songs. And the greatest challenge of them all, the one that is touching every part of the world, every home, every institution, every world issue is the woman's question.

The church cannot be a community as long as women remain invisible, rejected and reduced to consumers of the faith instead of being able to function as fully adult Christians in a community of disciples.

Women are most of the poor, most of the refugees, most of the uneducated, most of the beaten and most of the rejected of the world. They are also most of the exalted. On no other class, surely, has so much poetry, so much music, so many flowers, so much adulation, so much tolerance, so much romantic love and so little moral and intellectual, spiritual and human respect been lavished. Now we even read encyclicals of praise and apology about women which then invariably end by reiterating their "special" nature, an empty paean which translates to mean their separateness, their second-classness, their subservience, however nice the words. Where in that is the presence of Jesus to the homeless woman, to the beggar woman, to the abandoned woman, to the ministering woman, to the woman alone, to the woman whose questions, cries and life experience appear no place in the systems of the world and no place in the church as well?

Except of course to be defined once more as another kind of human, not quite as competent, not quite as valued, not quite as human, not quite as graced by God as men? Where in that is the discipleship of Jesus? Where in that is living in today's world as Jesus lived in his?

What does the theology of discipleship demand here? What does the theology of discipleship imply here? Are women simply half a disciple of Christ? To be half-commissioned, half-noticed, and half-valued? Or are women the other half of the church, without which the Christian community will never be whole and its discipleship will never be authentic?

In the light of these situations, there are, consequently, questions in the Christian community today that cannot be massaged by footnotes or obscured by jargon or made palatable by the

retreat to faith. On the contrary, before these issues, the footnotes falter, the language serves only to heighten the problem,
faith itself mocks the question. The discipleship of women is the
question that is not going to go away. Indeed, the discipleship of
the church in regard to women is the question that will, in the
long run, prove the church itself.

In the woman's question the church is facing one of its most
serious challenges to discipleship since the emergence of the
great and agonizing debates about slavery. Tradition, it seemed,
affirmed slavery; major philosophers had accepted slavery; an
apostle himself preached about slavery. But, in the light of new
evidence, under the scrutiny of new thinking, in the face of the
piercing example of Jesus, discipleship demanded something new,
demanded human freedom, demanded taking people in who had
once, by the will of God they said, been kept out.

The major question facing Christians today, too, is what discipleship means in a church that does not accept women as full
followers of Christ. If discipleship is reduced to maleness, what
does that do to the rest of the Christian dispensation? If only
men can really live discipleship to the fullest, what is the use of
a woman aspiring to discipleship at all? What does it mean for
the women themselves who are faced with rejection, devalua-
tion and a debatable theology based on the remnants of a bad
biology that has theologized women out of theology? What, as
well, does the rejection of women at the highest levels of the
church mean for the discipleship of men who claim to be enlightened but continue to support the very system that mocks
half the human race?

What does it mean for the church that claims to be a follower
of the Jesus who pulled asses out of ditches on the Sabbath and
cured women with an issue of blood? And finally what does
it mean for a society badly in need of a cosmic worldview at
the dawn of a global age? The answers are discouragingly clear
on all counts. Christian discipleship is not simply in danger of

being stunted. Discipleship has, in fact, become the enemy. The refusal to admit women to full discipleship—something the church itself teaches is required of us all—has become at least as problematic a matter for the integrity of the church as the open discussion of its possibility could ever be. The fact that those who are admitted to discipleship continue to exclude women from the offices of the church that shape its theology, guide its spiritual life and minister to its people, let alone from ordination itself, brings the very notion of discipleship itself into question. Women are beginning to wonder if discipleship has anything to do with them at all.

And therein lies the contemporary question of discipleship. Some consider faithfulness to the gospel to mean doing what we have always done. Others find faithfulness only in being what we have always been. The distinctions are crucial. The distinctions are also essential to the understanding of discipleship in the modern church.

When "the tradition" becomes synonymous with "the system" and maintaining the system becomes more important than maintaining the spirit of the tradition, discipleship shrivels. It becomes at best "obedience" or "fidelity" to the past but not necessarily a deep-down commitment to the presence of the living Christ confronting the leprosies of the age.

Bernard Lonergan in *Method in Theology* calls religious conversion an "other-worldly falling in love," the giving of the self to the will of God for the world. It is a love, in other words, that is unlike the love we see around us, grounded on different principles, illumined by a different light, meant to witness to something other than dominance and difference and the idolatry of maleness. Discipleship that surrenders to the presence of Christ in life, presumes from each of us, from the church itself, that same kind of reckless, open, receiving, giving love that Jesus brought to the blind on the roads of Galilee, to the body of a dead girl, to the plea of the menstruating woman. Society called the blind sinful, a female child useless, the woman unclean, all of them marginal to the system, condemned to the fringes of life, excluded from the center of the synagogue, barred from the heart of the Temple. But Jesus takes each of them to himself, despite the laws, regardless of the culture, notwithstanding the disapproval of the spiritual notables of the area and fills them with himself. To be disciples of Jesus means that we must do the same. There are some things, it seems, that brook no rationalizing for the sake of institutional niceties. Discipleship infers, implies, requires no less than the love of Jesus for everyone, everywhere regardless of who would draw limits around the love of God.

Discipleship and faith are of a piece. To say that we believe that God loves the poor, judges in their behalf, wills their deliverance but do nothing ourselves to free the poor, to hear their pleas, to lift their burdens, to act in their behalf is an empty faith indeed. To say that God is love and not ourselves love as God loves may well be church but it is not Christianity. To say that all persons are equal in God's sight and ourselves maintain a theology of inequality, a spirituality of domination in the name of God is to live a lie.

Discipleship recognizes the face of the Divine, the blessing, in what the world calls burden and unmasks in what we call burdens their blessing to us all. But if discipleship is the following of Jesus, beyond all bounds, at all costs, for the bringing of the Reign of God, for the establishment of right relationships, then to ground a woman's calling to follow Christ in her ability to look like Jesus obstructs the very thing the church is founded to do. It obstructs a woman's ability to follow Christ to the full. And it does it for the sake of religion and in defiance of the gospel itself. How can a church such as this call convincingly to the world in the name of justice to practice a justice it does not practice itself? How is it that the church can call institutions to deal with women as full human beings made in the image of God when their humanity is precisely what the church itself holds against them? In the name of God. It is a philosophical question of immense proportions. It is the question which, like slavery, brings the church to the test.

For the church to be present to the woman's question, to minister to it, to be disciple to it, the church must itself become converted to the issue. In fact, the church must become converted by the issue. Men who do not take the woman's issue seriously may be good priests and kind husbands and caring brothers and faithful friends but they cannot possibly be disciples. They cannot possibly be "other Christs": Not the Christ born of a woman. Not the Christ who commissioned women to preach him. Not the Christ who took faculties from a woman at Cana. Not the Christ who sent women to preach resurrection to apostles who would not believe it. Not the Christ who sent the Holy Spirit on Mary the woman as well as Peter the man.

If this is the Jesus whom we as Christians, as church, are to follow, then the discipleship of the church is now mightily in question.

Indeed, when the poet Basho writes, "I do not seek to follow in the footsteps of those of old. I seek the things they sought," the insight sears the Christian soul as well. Genuine discipleship is not a matter of historical repetition. It depends for its authenticity on our bringing the will of God for humankind to the questions of this age as Jesus did to his. As long as tradition is used to mean following in the footsteps of our past rather than seeking to follow the spirit of Christ, it is unlikely that we will preserve more than the shell of the church. The very consistency of the faith will be shattered beyond repair. Baptism and Eucharist, full for half of us but not for all of us, will be a sham. We will have preserved pieces of the past in the name of discipleship to the detriment of the fullness of Christianity in the present.

Humanity across differences has become the thread that binds the world together in a global age. What was once a hierarchy of humankind is coming to be seen for what it is: the oppression of humankind. The colonization of women is as unacceptable now as the colonial oppression of Africa, the Crusades against Turks, the enslavement of blacks and the decimation of Indians in the name of God. The humanization of the human race is upon us. The only question for the church is whether the humanization of the human race will lead as well to the Christianization of the Christian church. Otherwise, discipleship will die and the integrity of the church with it.

We must take discipleship seriously or we shall leave the church of the future with functionaries, perhaps, but certainly without disciples. The fact is that Christianity lives in Christians, not in books, not in documents, not in platitudes. Discipleship to women and the discipleship of women is key to the discipleship of the church. The questions are clear. The answer may, at this point, seem obscure and uncertain but the conclusion is not merely academic; it is crucial to the future of the church; it is the essence of discipleship; it is the ultimate measure of Christianity.

4.

Wanted: The Other Half of the Church

I hear the statement "I was raised Catholic" more often than I like these days. Too often, it seems to me, it means that someone formed in the faith no longer identifies with it. Too often many of these people are women. Middle-aged women. Young women. Women on whom the future of the transmission of the faith depends.

At one time to say "I was raised Catholic" had the ring of the pedestrian to it. After all, so many of us were. In a Catholic immigrant population, to be raised Catholic communicated a person's cultural identity as much as it marked their convictions. It bore the stamp of national pride and political meaning, as much as it denoted a set of religious beliefs. To be raised Catholic had something to do with a person's whole identity.

But even then, the words carried a particular spiritual connotation for everyone. For me, they meant that I went to Catholic schools and haunted Catholic churches like a small ghost. In those days churches were never locked until sometime after dark and children could do such things with impunity. I did it all the time. I hunted churches down, tugged at the great wooden doors that signaled their entrance into another world and escaped into the cool, damp dark inside. There was something there for me that touched a quiet, inner place that was touchable by nothing else on earth.

I would skate around a neighborhood corner and run right into one after another of them—Hungarian, Polish, German, Irish parishes—all catering to their own kind, all the same and all slightly different. They existed to revere differences, to acknowledge distinct histories and cultural customs. At each place, I would take off my skates on the church steps, hide them in the bushes outside and tip-toe down one dark church aisle after another, smelling the candles, studying the windows, struggling to read the Latin inscriptions that circled the frescoes over the altars. I was a Catholic through and through. In the church I felt safe. I felt at home. Something here both catechized and completed me.

It took years before I began to realize, as have a number of other women, that the fact is that a woman is not completely "at home" in the church, at all. In fact, her "completeness" may be more in question here than any other place in society. Her catechesis—that God is love, that God created all of us in God's own image, that women, as well as men, are fully human—remains always problematic.

The words "I was raised Catholic" have a particular connotation for women. A woman discovers over time that there is a difference between being raised in the faith and being part of the church. As the years go by, it becomes clear: Women get the faith; men get the church to go with it.

That's the way things are, we hear. That's all there is to it. That was the way God means it to be.

For centuries, the social parallels that developed out of that kind of theology were obvious. Women were simply expected to take the ancillary role God had decreed for them, everywhere, at all times, in all situations: in marriage, in politics, in business, in professional arenas, in the home and definitely in the church.

But the last half of the twentieth century, devoted to the human sciences, awash in biological and genetic data, began slowly but surely to give the lie to those ideas, to suspect the rationale for those ideas, to shatter that assumption from one arena to the next. Theologically, the notion was even more suspect: What kind of a God was it that made humanity of two types: one superior, one inferior; one godly, one not?

Around us, every other organization in the western world teetered on a consciousness of the fact that its composition mirrored only half the human race, listened to only half the human race, respected the insights of only half the human race, incorporated into itself the ideas and directions and agendas of only half the human race. But not the church.

As all these other institutions and organizations restructured themselves to remedy what was clearly an aberration of the human condition, a distortion of both theology and scripture, the church alone failed to address the issue as a major theological question in its own right. Instead, women were told that the church was a Divine institution set up by Jesus himself to keep women at a distance from all things sacred. The apostles were all men, we were told repeatedly—as if the Twelve Apostles, symbolic Christian surrogates for the Twelve Tribes of Israel, were the only ministers in the church. No mention of Mary who bore Jesus, or of Mary Magdalene and the women of Israel who were the first to support Jesus "out of their own sustenance," or of the Samaritan woman to whom Jesus revealed himself as Messiah before having said a word to Peter, or of the women who labored with Paul to build the early church. No mention at all of them, of the women disciples of Jesus, of women in their own right. Nothing.

But then, astounding things, life-changing things, began to happen. Pope John XXIII, in his encyclical *Pacem in terris,* listed the woman's issue as one of the "signs of the times," along with poverty and nuclearism. Vatican II issued a document on the vocation of the laity, and made no distinction between lay men and lay women. New liturgical norms eliminated the altar rail and allowed women entry into the sanctuary, the Holy of Holies, alongside male lectors and male ministers of the Eucharist and male altar servers. Communion in the hand, with its clear implication that women as well as men were worthy to touch the consecrated host, became a commonplace.

Apostolicam actuositatem, the *Document on the Laity,* said it directly: "Since in our times women have an ever more active share in the whole life of society, it is very important that they participate more widely also in the various fields of the church's apostolate" (AA, 9).

And for a while it looked as if they would. Male universities began to admit women to degrees in the sacred sciences on a par with men, in the same classes, under the same academic requirement. Lay ecclesial ministry programs began to emerge everywhere. By the year 2002, US universities had graduated over 34,000 lay ministers, two out of every three of them women, only 3 percent of them women religious. Under their aegis, lay women, too, became theologians, canonists, liturgists and parish administrators.

Clearly, even the church was beginning to flirt with the possibility that women were an idea whose time had come.

Finally, for the first time in history, in 1985, a pope wrote an encyclical on women. It is a gracious letter and a fulsome one. Nevertheless, the encyclical, *Mulieris dignitatem,* continues to imply the notion of a separate or dual anthropology: that man, the male, is one kind of human but woman is another. That biological differences have something to do with spiritual differences. That Jesus who became "flesh" became one kind of flesh that apparently does not include the other kind. Ten years later, however, Pope John Paul II carved out another new moment in the history of women in the church when he wrote a letter of apology to the women of the world for failures of the church in the past to recognize the equality and value of women. He wrote, "Such respect (for women) must first and foremost be won through an effective and intelligent campaign for the promotion of women, concentrating on all areas of women's life and beginning with a universal recognition of the dignity of women." Accent on "effective and intelligent campaign for the promotion of women" and "on all areas of women's life." Surely here was the beginning of a new world for us all. And for a while it seemed to be true.

Dioceses everywhere, in response to the documents of Vatican II and encouraged by papal support, began to include women on boards, in chanceries, in parish administrative positions.

Parishes accepted women into liturgical ministries: little girls began to be altar servers alongside little boys; women read from the scriptures at Mass; lay eucharistic ministers, women as well as men, served homes for the aged, hospitals, and at regular liturgical celebrations.

Congregations began to take for granted that women would also serve in new kinds of parish work. Lay programs gave degrees in pastoral ministry, theology and theological studies, divinity, religious studies, spirituality and pastoral counseling. Now marriage preparation conferences were as easily staffed by women as by men. Liturgical planning, adult catechesis, parish organizational activities and decision-making positions on parish boards became common for women as well as for men.

Most significant of all, perhaps, the church began to change the language of liturgical events to include the recognition of women as part of the assembly.

Discussions began in theological circles about the theological possibility of the restoration of the diaconate for women as it had been for men.

Women, it seemed, had finally arrived as full adult members of the church. They were now in the language of prayer, in the offices of the diocese and on the altars of parish churches. Barely, perhaps, but there, nevertheless. Now it was only a matter of new practices becoming ordinary before women would be taken for granted as leaders in the church and bearers of the spirit. Both the Fatherhood and the Motherhood of God were slowly coming into consciousness, into public view.

Then, slowly but surely, the reversal began. The "program" the pope called for died a rude and insidious death. Almost imperceptibly, at first, new statements began to be released, most of them with little fanfare but far-reaching results. The doors, one at a time, began to close.

Seminarians were directed in *Pastores dabo vobis* in 1993 to have priests as their spiritual directors, despite years of being free to choose whomever suited them best: men or women. Clearly the men of the church had nothing to learn from the women of the church. That door closed.

Word leaked out, of course, of seminarians who asked their women directors to continue with them regardless. But the system itself stayed sterile, untouched by the feminine dimension of the mystical and a barren place indeed. Now some researchers estimate the life span of a new priest to be five years.

Sister Carmel McEnroy was peremptorily removed from seminary teaching despite years of outstanding teacher evaluations. The charge against her was that she signed a statement asking the church to open a discussion on the ordination of women. One by one, teaching positions in theology closed to women. In some cases the exclusion was more subtle. Women were simply relegated to elective areas of theology programs so that traditional ideas, male ideas, could never be broadened to include the insights or questions of women on subjects of theological substance. Another door closed.

A woman religious with a certification in clinical pastoral education gave years of free service in hospital ministry. When a vacancy arose, she asked the local bishop to hire her as Catholic chaplain. He refused. That door closed. In the end, she was hired by the hospital itself as "ecumenical chaplain"—which, ironically, makes her doubly effective in her work. She meets more patients, gives more spiritual consolation, is respected by more people. But, at the same time, she remains officially unacknowledged by the Catholic community whose faith informs her ministry. In the meantime, she answers every emergency call in the deep of the night and then phones rectory after rectory in an attempt to get priests to administer the Sacrament of Anointing of the Sick to Catholic patients.

Altar girls have come to be more and more rare rather than more and more common. Some dioceses forbid them altogether and without apology, let alone the grace to blush. Apparently the church against whom the gates of hell cannot prevail can be brought to perdition by little eleven-year-old girls. With this door closing goes the commitment of many of the women of the next generation.

In diocese after diocese, where they have served in official capacities for years, women are being removed from every office in the chancery except, perhaps, as vicars for religious. And at the same time, new documents, notably the "Instruction on Certain Questions Regarding the Collaboration of the Non-Ordained Faithful" of 1997, remind priests that they hold the ultimate authority in every dimension of church and parish life, regardless of their lack of experience or professional preparation in any of them. In those cases, the doors to any kind of official hearing of the issues or concerns of women have closed soundly and completely.

One by one, inner-city parishes find themselves discontinued for lack of priests or served only by men too old, too tired themselves to do more than say an occasional Mass. But women, even those with degrees in lay ecclesial ministry programs, who ask to be allowed to serve those parishes get no welcome. So, the parishes disappear silently where the congregations are too small, too old, or too poor to have their protests heard. This is not without consequences. Many of the women, after years of trying to serve the church and being rebuffed, disappear with those churches—to other work, to other churches, or to no church at all. And they are taking their daughters with them. Faced with a choice between maleness and the sacraments in a sacramental church, the church is choosing for maleness.

According to the Center for Applied Research in the Apostolate (CARA), in 1965 in the United States, 549 parishes were without a resident priest. In 2002, there were 2,929 US parishes without a resident priest. Around the world, those figures had risen from 94,846 priestless parishes in 1980, the first year in which data began to be collected on a global scale, to 105,530 parishes in the year 2000.

Bishop Raymond Lucker of New Ulm, Wisconsin, now deceased, loved to tell the story of his attempt to maintain the traditional parish structures in the face of the dwindling number of priests. His solution was to assign a priest to three parishes at a time, a kind of circuit-rider ecclesiology. The priest would reside in the largest of the three parishes, but preside at the weekly Sunday liturgy for the other two, as well. Women religious acted as residential parish administrators in the parishes that had no daily access to a priest. After several years of this arrangement, Lucker decided it was unfair for one parish to have continual access to a priest while the other two did not. He decreed that the priest would move from parish to parish every three years. Suddenly, he reported, the mail started pouring in asking him not to do that. The underlying message in all of them brooked no doubt: "We haven't had this kind of parish activity for years," the letters said. "We don't want a priest. Just leave Sister where she is."

But every day that kind of joint ministry fades, those doors close. Universities report that of the records they have on the ministerial positions of their graduates, most now occupy volunteer positions in catechetical programs.

The diaconate program, now restored for men only, has grown to over 12,000 ordained deacons since its inception. But the thought of even discussing the restoration of the diaconate program for women, too—an institutional staple in both the Eastern and the Western churches for ten centuries—has been dismissed without consideration in the document *Institutionis diaconorum permanentiarum* on the grounds that it could lead to the expectation of priestly ordination for women. Despite the fact that the same argument is not used in regard to married men. Nor can ordained deacons do anything that any other lay person cannot do without permission—except, of course, maintain the male character of a sacramental church.

Finally, in what may be the most subversive move of all, new documents—notably *Liturgiam authenticam* in 2001—completely obliterate female references from the prayers and hymns of the church, even in scriptures clearly addressed to the whole Christian community, let alone in references to the infinite, unknowable and totally spiritual Godhead who has been made completely captive to maleness. The door to existence for women, even in the pronouns of the church, has been closed.

Philosophers and social psychologists alike know that what is missing in the language is missing in the mind and what is missing in the mind will never be embodied in the structures of a people, a culture, an organization, a church. Whom we do not address in a conversation does not exist for us. Language is not a trivial issue. Language is the ultimate delete.

And the question is why? Why all these exclusions in the face of a Council of the church that called for equality, an encyclical on the gifting nature of women, a papal letter of apology for the past sins of the church against women and the promise of "programs, etc.?" Why these sudden reversals of practice in a church that had found new life, new energy, new witness in the world as a result of its long overdue recognition of the full humanity of women? The clear but new awareness of the implications for the church of the gospel descriptions of Jesus with women? The theological significance of a creation story that insists on the common human identity of both Adam and Eve: "bone of my bone; flesh of my flesh." Somebody, Adam recognizes, who is just like himself. Where is the "campaign for the promotion of women, concentrating on all areas of women's life and beginning with a universal recognition of the dignity of women" promised by this pope that will promote the advancement of women in the church as well as in all other sectors of society?

Why do we have thousands of priestless parishes, thousands fewer seminarians and, at the same time, thousands of unemployed lay ministers—most of them women—unless it is more preferable to close parishes than to allow women to maintain the very life blood of a communal church.

What can we conclude? That the papal letter to women lacks integrity? That the Council has been hijacked? That papal messages are routinely ignored by those who claim to accept them? It is a question of great ethical and ecclesiastical import. On it may well rest not only the renewal of the church but its future, as well: its future effectiveness, its future witness—its very impact on the future of the world—as secular society, rather than the church, leads the world to a new understanding of creation.

5.

Mary

Perhaps the most revealing thing I can say to anybody in an article about Marian devotions is that I myself never had any. At least not for most of my life. In those two statements may lie both the age-old quandary of Mary's place in personal spiritual development and a hint of the continuing impact of Mary of Nazareth throughout the ages.

Mary of Nazareth, as my generation received her in the 1950s and 1960s, held no interest for me. She was not my mother's kind of woman. She was also not the kind of woman my mother was raising me to be. In an era of newly emerging women professionals, in a culture where a college education began to be as common for a woman as for a man, in a country where the legal rights of women even in marriage were becoming a subject of debate, in a society coming awake to Simone de Beauvoir's *The Second Sex*, the image of the passive, invisible woman struck my generation, if not passé, as at least suspect. Religious as well as secular feminists began to point out that classic conceptions of the role and person of Mary were at best really male images of women idealized. Where I myself was concerned, the figures of Teresa of Avila, Catherine of Siena, Joan of Arc—women who were adults in their own right, women who made a contribution to the spiritual life, women who got things done—meant more.

Clearly, devotion to Mary of Nazareth, the mother of Jesus, is not a subject that begins and ends with the liturgies, the prayers or the traditions of the church. Devotion to Mary is not decided by theological formulations alone. When Carl Jung explored the relationship between psychology and religion, and with it the value of veneration for Mary to the human psyche, scholars of both religion and psychology raised their eyebrows in surprise, if not disbelief. What did devotion to Mary, an often discredited concept of Roman Catholicism, have to do either with psychology or with the role of faith in contemporary life? But Jung was not cautious in his conclusions. In fact, Jung may have understood the role of Marian devotion in Christian theology and human development in ways, perhaps, that other writers in the field did not.

Mary, Jung made clear, was not simply a woman shrouded in anonymity, lost to time and lacking in import. Jung wrote: "Mary was the instrument of God's birth and so became involved in the trinitarian drama as a human being. The Mother of God can, therefore, be regarded as a symbol of [hu]mankind's essential participation in the Trinity." She was, in other words, a bridge, an archetype, a sign, a symbol of the female energy in a God that had, despite the best theological definitions of the nature of God, become too male, too distant, too much judge, too little mother.

Devotion to Mary took on a new focus through a new lens. Jung uncovered what any serious review of the history of devotion to Mary would surely suggest: Mary was as important to the understanding of human development as she was to the theological constructs of the church and, just as surely, she was as important to the theological constructs of the church as she was to any kind of personal piety or human maturation.

It is not surprising, then, that Mary has never been a nonfigure in Christianity. If anything, she has at some periods of history been more central to Christian sentiment than Jesus. What's more, she has always been as much a subject of theological discourse as she was a rendering of personal holiness.

Biblical information on the person and life of Mary of Nazareth is sparse enough to be almost lacking but her very status as the mother of Jesus makes her a formidable theological personage: What was the human and spiritual effect of this motherhood on her? On humankind in general? On the church? On the role and place and nature of women in particular?

Historical answers to those questions are wide ranging. In fact, vestiges of each are with us still. But not simply in theological tomes. Popular devotions express the *sensus fidelium,* the theological sense or understanding of the faithful, in regard to the place and person of Mary in Christian life. Some of these images of Mary have faded with time. Others persist whatever official documents or scholarly interpretations say to contradict them. And it is in popular devotion that we see best the truth that while theology must inform devotion, that devotion must be informed by popular devotion, as well.

Two images of Mary emerge early in the history of the church. The first, embodied in the infancy narratives of scripture, stresses the idea of her virginal conception of Jesus. The second, the notion of Mary's role as mediator, as suppliant, between the needs of people and the throne of God arises as early as the fourth or, some say, even the third century. Whether or not, as some scholars argue, this concept derives from the lingering strains of goddess worship transformed into Christian terms is interesting but not the only warrant for the idea. The fact is that the definition of Mary as "Mother of God" by the Council of Ephesus in 431 legitimated the question theologically. After all, if Jesus is both God and human as Ephesus proclaims and Mary is the mother of Jesus, then Mary is also "Theotokos," Mother of God. Whether or not Mary has special intercessory power by virtue of her motherhood alone becomes, then, a constant question in the history of the church, right down to the time of Vatican II.

Patristic theologians—Irenaeus, Justin Martyr, Tertullian and Ambrose, in particular—added another dimension to the nature of Marian devotion. Given to finding "types" in scripture that spoke on the level of the metaphorical or symbolic as well as on the literal, they defined Mary as "the new Eve." Irenaeus' doctrine of "recirculation," the notion that evil is reversed in the same manner in which it came to be, made a convincing, and lasting, argument for Mary as prototype of the obedient woman. Eve, by this time, the scapegoat for a sin that was Adam's as well as Eve's, pales in her sight. Mary, this theology postulates, by her obedience to the will of God "redeems" women—humankind— from the burden of degrading sinfulness. In the new Adam, Jesus—and the new Eve, Mary—the world begins again. Mary is clearly a "type" of Eve and so a central figure in the Christian story, a commanding figure in the spiritual life.

Not surprisingly, then, by the Middle Ages, devotions based on Mary's intercessory power as miraculous Virgin, Mother of God, and new Eve—as instrument of salvation, God-bearer and sinless one—grew to exaggerated proportions. Mary came to be seen as the gentling hand of heaven in hard times. If God was remote from the people, if Latin liturgies distanced worshipers from the sacramental life of the church, if scripture had no place in their lives, Mary nevertheless stayed accessible. Mary, they knew, was human, real, understanding—a mother. She was the compassion- ate one. God they saw in the midst of the plague as the harsh judge whose mind could be changed by her and her alone.

The Middle Ages became a Marian Age. Other devotions dimmed in comparison. Songs, prayers and litanies stressed her saving power, her intermediary influence, her heavenly central- ity. It's in the Middle Ages that Marian antiphons are written which survive to this day. In this period, the Hail Mary becomes popular. And in this era, too, the Rosary begins to supplant the

Divine Office, its Hail Marys substituting for the psalms. By this time, Mary is revered and appealed to at least as much as Jesus, if not more. But the counteraction was yet to come.

In the sixteenth century, Martin Luther and the Reformers also made Mary a central point in theology. But they questioned her centrality, her titles, the theological concepts—mediator of all graces, queen of heaven, co-redeemer of humankind—that were springing up in her behalf. They argued that Jesus Christ alone ranks as mediator between God and humankind.

The point made good theological disputation, perhaps, but bad Reformation politics. Instead of restraining theological fervor for the role of the Mother of God in the heart of the faith, Mary became a defining point in Catholicism. By the seventeenth century, Protestant churches had all but eliminated any reference to Mariology whatsoever. For Catholics, on the other hand, devotion to Mary became a distinguishing feature of the tradition.

Whole religious congregations were dedicated to the name and honor of Mary. Commitment to her service became a mark of spirituality. Louis-Marie Grignon de Montfort (d. 1716) developed a Marian spirituality that required people to become "slaves of Mary." All favors were obtained by her from God, he argued; all actions were to be in her service. Now Mary had complete power over God. It was a devotion that reached all the way to my novitiate.

At first, I was secretly embarrassed to be so spiritually unaffected—even disconcerted—by the implications of such theology. As the years went by, however, I became more and more convinced that those concerns were not without merit, however much devotion to Mary marked the spirituality of the church itself. Nor was I alone in my dis-ease.

The Enlightenment era of the eighteenth century with its emphasis on reason dampened, at least for a while, the emotional excess that had crept into Marian devotion in Counter-Reformation times. Nineteenth-century Romanticism, however, with its emphasis on feelings, introduced a new surge of both popular and ecclesiastical recognition that shaped twentieth-century devotion, as well. Apparition sites, the most famous of which were Lourdes, Guadalupe, Fatima and, by the end of the century, Medjugorje, became places of pilgrimage. Marian sodalities and May devotions became popular everywhere. The Nine First Saturdays in honor of Mary ranked along with the Nine First Fridays in privilege and indulgences. Mary—the passive, quiet, unquestioning Mary—became the Catholic girls' model of Catholic womanhood. And finally, the declaration of two Marian dogmas—her Immaculate Conception in 1854 and her Assumption into heaven in 1950—crowned centuries of Marian devotion with official recognition of her spiritual importance and stature.

And yet, something else had happened in the twentieth century, as well. A new consciousness of the equality, full humanity and social role of women swept the globe. Governments passed laws guaranteeing women civil rights, education, pay equity, legal protection and equal participation in local, national and international governing bodies. Women in the church became theologians, scripture scholars, liturgists and writers. Clearly, women had become anything but passive, quiet and invisible.

With the changes in women themselves came the discovery of a Mary who had been anything but simply a pawn of the system. Theologians of the rank of Karl Rahner as well as a new generation of women scholars began to see something very different in the story of Mary than had been defined before them.

New litanies in her name talked about her strength of mind, her willingness to confront systems, her prophetic witness to the life and work of Jesus, as well as her presence at Pentecost—with everything that implied. Women—I myself—began to see a Mary emerge in scripture who was as called by God to save the people as Moses and Abraham had ever been. This Mary, I began to realize, was independent and strong. She was a woman who knew exile. She had braved social rejection for the sake of the will of God. She knew suffering and poverty and powerlessness, just as women everywhere did. But she was a woman who never gave in to institutional restrictions and never gave up her right to shape her world. This was a woman who never doubted the Word of God for her, whatever the system said to the contrary. She had debated with angels. She had asked no male, neither Joseph nor the high priests, for permission to do what she knew God was calling her to do. Through her, the will of God was turned into the body and blood of Jesus. Through her visit to Elizabeth, she supported other women in their own call. Through her faith, faith grew. She directed the ministry of Jesus at the Wedding Feast of Cana. She sang the Magnificat of Liberation. She believed all the way to the cross and then went on beyond it.

All of a sudden, it became very clear. Mary was the feminine energy in Christianity. That's why every age was drawn to her. That's why no age has abandoned her. That's why both men and women find the missing piece of Christianity in her.

Indeed theological concerns abound: How much devotion to Mary is too much devotion? Which elements of the image and ministry of Mary are still missing in Christianity? What is her rightful, her determining place in Christian life and spirituality? The struggle to define goes on to this day. The movement to grant Mary the titles of Coredemptrix and Mediatrix of all graces has gained new impetus under the papacy of John Paul II, despite the narrow decision of the Council fathers of Vatican II to table such a motion.

But history is clear: it doesn't much matter what kind of official definitions of Mary obtain, in the end, it's the *sensus fidelium,* the awareness in the heart of the faithful that Mary is at the heart of the tradition, which, as it has in the past, will certainly prevail.

6.

The Visitation

On Thanksgiving Day, 2008, a popular ABC TV morning news show featured the story of the mother of a 22-year-old soldier who had been killed in Iraq. Part of a supply convoy servicing the perimeter of Baghdad, his Humvee had been hit by an explosion-rigged vehicle. Just days after his twenty-second birthday, the young man and two of his best friends were dead, the other, permanently brain damaged.

His mother, reading the diary returned in his army trunk, discovered the names of the friends who had been killed and wounded with him. Then she searched the United States until she found their mothers. They came from across the country to meet together now, these women. They hear one another's stories. They share a common bond.

In their mutual pain, these women have found both support and understanding. "There is no difference in our grief. It's absolutely painful," Doris said. "There is nothing in the world that is going to bring our boys back, but we have each other." For this small bit of shared humanity, for this cocoon of emotional

---

Eds.—This reflection was inspired by a painting, "The Visitation," by artist Janet McKenzie.

safety, for this personal place of support in their grief and the hope of sustenance it brought for the future, they were thankful.

It is, I think, the same story Janet McKenzie is begging the world to see in her painting, "The Visitation."

The unique dimension of the story of this painting is that it's not unique at all. It's a universal one. But it has been invisible for far too long. Now, in our day, science has finally exposed and defined it.

"Artists treat facts as stimuli for imagination," Arthur Koestler wrote, "whereas scientists use imagination to coordinate facts." The real social impact comes when the two—art and science— merge into one awareness, into one great impulse toward a newer, more conscious way of being.

When artists discover one of the hidden determinants of life intuitively and scientists discover the origin of it experientially, the world of quarks and clones, parallel universes and cosmic expansion becomes a more readable story of the miracle of what it means to be alive. Of what it means, in the midst of interplanetary reality, to live our own small private lives.

When the artist and the scientist collaborate to discover another of the undercurrents of what it means to be human, life takes on a new level of spiritual evolution. Then we understand ourselves better. Then we understand life better. Then we understand better what it is we are meant to be. Then we recognize the ways of God better.

In our own time, it has happened. In fact, you see it before your very eyes—both in this painting of a time past and in the world around us now.

Janet McKenzie's "The Visitation" haunted me for days. There was simply lurking in it, behind the obvious, more, I thought, than the common awareness of the binding female power of pregnancy.

The fact that women share a common life-giving experience in the very chemistry of their bodies—whether they themselves ever experience pregnancy or not—is commonplace. The very word "woman" rings of "wombness" for many. But the haunting look on the faces of "The Visitation" say more. Much more.

The faces of Mary and Elizabeth, dark and somber, thoughtful and aware, in McKenzie's "The Visitation" say something far beyond either the exultation of pregnancy or the creative power of it. This is not a picture about the delirium of motherhood. There is a storm stirring in the hearts of these women—deep and different than most at such a moment as this, something epochal and eruptive. The facts of this pregnancy are clearly different than the simple, natural dimensions of it.

This pregnancy, "The Visitation" implies, says that these two particular pregnancies are changing life in ways no pregnancy before them ever implied. These women, the picture is clear, are bound together in ways far beyond the physical. This pregnancy says that both the older woman—for whom pregnancy means a need for more vigorous energy than her years would commonly allow—and the younger woman—for whom a first pregnancy means new stature in the human community—are bound by something far more impacting than gestation.

The picture captures a moment in time—full of awareness, heavy with universal meaning. These two women know that what they are about to go through is not really two separate moments of life at all. The very act of pregnancy binds them together, yes, but it binds them to all of life differently, as well. It has not only changed them but it is about to change the history of the world. It is of them, of course, and it is far outside and beyond them at the same time.

This is life beyond their own small lives that they are facing now. This is life layers above the physical, oceans below the conscious.

And that's where science comes in.

Women scholars have for long now pointed out that at the moment of change, in the face of awesome, perhaps even terrifying awareness of her situation, Mary does not go to the men in her life for support. She does not go to her fiancé, Joseph, for understanding. She does not go to her father for protection. She does not go to the priests of the Temple for vindication. No, Mary goes to another woman. Mary, the pregnant but unwed woman, travels to the hill country to be with her old cousin

Elizabeth, who is also pregnant, also dealing with overwhelming change and the isolating implications of it in her life.

None of it, the two women knew and the academic world realized over the centuries, made any human sense. After all, to be unmarried and pregnant in the Middle East of that time—in fact, in many parts of the Middle East even at this time—is dangerous space for a woman. She can be driven out of the family. She will certainly be forever disgraced. She can be stoned to death.

So, it seems sensible to wonder, why go to another woman, an old woman, who can herself do nothing to save her, who has no power to make the social situation better?

But to a woman it makes sense. Seeking the support of another woman in the midst of struggle has made emotional sense to women for centuries. And now it makes scientific sense, as well.

The science of women—women doing science—has finally opened new insights for all of us into what it means to be human. It gives the whole human community another way of reacting to life under pressure. It provides the world with a whole new way of looking at women and what women have to offer a world certain that its security lies in, as the psalmist says, "bows and shields, in carriages and horses"—in armies and nuclear weapons.

Now, thanks to a newly released and benchmark study, science and art come together in one great monumental moment that can make pain easier for all of us to bear.

According to principal investigator Shelley E. Taylor of a UCLA study, "Behavioral Responses to Stress," covered in *Science Daily*, "For decades, psychological research maintained that both men and women rely on fight or flight to cope with stress—meaning that when confronted by stress, individuals either react with aggressive behavior, such as verbal conflict and more drastic actions, or withdraw from the stressful situation."

But, these researchers discovered, the participants in the five decades of research that consistently confirmed the "fight or flight theory" were primarily men. The UCLA study, using women rather than men for the first time in the history of the study of stress research, discovered that "fight or flight" is not the primary or normal response of women. Instead, science now understands, women under stress "tend and befriend." They gather with other women to construct other means of dealing with conflict and pressure, rather than aggressive ones. Women, under stress, they found, take care of one another. They take care of children. They continue to concentrate on the functioning and development of the human community. They bring stability to situations of tumult and confusion.

The female hormone oxytocin, unlike the male hormone testosterone, the researchers tell us, steadies a person, brings order into bedlam, binds women together in support groups to keep the world operating in hard times. It is an indispensable element of the human condition; it is an essential component of social growth. It is plain proof, to both art and science, that to eliminate women from the great judgments and strategies of church and state is to rob the world of another way of responding to the kinds of stress that threaten its survival.

Now science knows what scripture and art, women and society, have known for eons. Mary and Elizabeth, Doris and the mothers of her son's now dead soldier friends—women everywhere—calm the chaos of the world. They show us all another way to be in the midst of the daily maelstroms of life. They help us survive. They bind us together to carry each other, to carry the human community, to allow others to carry us when we cannot carry ourselves.

To look at McKenzie's "The Visitation" is to look at an alternative world. It is to define the role of women in a new way. It gives new dignity and meaning to the friendship of women. It gives us all reason to believe that there can be another way through conflict other than force.

7.

God Our Father, God Our Mother

In Search of the Divine Feminine

There is a subject intimately connected to every religion that we are seldom willing to consider. And, if we do, we almost never talk about it out loud. The unknown or unspoken subject that lingers around the edge of thought in this new and cosmic age now is the subject of the feminine dimension of God: Is there any such thing, we wonder? And if there is, are we allowed to consider it? And if not, why not? Yet the truth is that what we think of the Divine Feminine will determine what we think about everything else in life. It grips us on both levels of humanity—the personal and the spiritual—and the effects of it are all around us. Women everywhere are denied positions in public arenas, excluded from religion's "Holy of Holies," undervalued, underrepresented, underpaid, and largely underdeveloped in social arenas.

The first level of impact is clearly theological. Now this is soul-searing and sober spiritual stuff! Is it heresy, we worry, even to put those two words together? Can we possibly, with good conscience, even say it: the Divine Feminine? If we ever do dare to say it, will we possibly get out of the church alive before a paddy wagon full of priests, ministers, popes and potentates snatch us up and take us away? The second level of the question is a profoundly personal one. It has to do with a breathtaking outbreak of spiritual imagination in women—with entirely new images of spiritual development among women—and the effect of these on roles, relationships, religions, and the definition of human rights, all dearly to be wished perhaps but certain to be contested.

The subject is a tangled, thorny, exhilarating and highly suspect excursion into the very center of the spiritual life and interfaith understanding. It is precisely this subject that explains both our personal spiritual development and our place as moral, spiritual, political and professional leaders in a world sorely in need of new forms of leadership everywhere. Why is the concept of the Divine Feminine important? The implications of this question shake the spiritual ground under our feet. In the attempt to lay out the dimensions of the subject, however, I found myself haunted by a story—at first seemingly irrelevant to this topic, but, at the same time, down deep, revelatory of the impact and import of this issue, not only to our spiritual life but to our daily life, as well.

In the story a tribal Elder is explaining to a child the nature of life: "Remember, child," the Elder teaches, "there are two wolves fighting for dominance within each of us. One wolf is good and the other wolf is evil." "But, Elder," the youngster asks, "which wolf will win?" The Elder answers, "It depends, dear child, on which wolf you feed." The story is clear: Who we become as persons depends on what we decide to develop in ourselves, in us and around us. Neurologists tell us now that it is experience that forges our brain patterns. What we think depends on what happens to us. We are not born as we are, we become it. What we believe derives from what we experience. The relationship of this story to the importance of the Divine Feminine in our own lives is obvious: First, if we fail to nourish the fullness of life in us, male and female, as the tribal Elder implies—both the feminine and the masculine side—in both women and men, the lack of that inclusiveness will warp our personalities and stunt the growth of our souls. Second, it is useless to say that we truly embrace the feminine dimension of life but refuse to be part of the public process that makes respect for the feminine an equally important part of the social fabric.

Newspapers ask, Can a woman really be president? Magazine articles ask, What makes a real man? Researchers ask, Are women and men different or the same? Theologians ask, Can a woman really image God? We ask, How does God really deal with women? Face-to-face or only through male or clerical intermediaries? For example, take our public language: Eskimos have forty words for snow. They see forty different kinds of snow. It's important to them to make the distinctions between them because snow is the very context of their lives. We have the same snow, yet we see only one kind, name one kind, because it's not as important to us. However, we have forty words for dog—we call them shepherds, poodles, chihuahuas. We have forty words for car—Kia, hatchback, SUV, limousine, convertible. But we have only two words for the human race—one of which we collapse into the other.

We are still teaching our children that when the gender of a group is clear, we may use the appropriate male or female pronoun. "Everyone attending the Women's Athletic Club presented her card," for instance. But when the gender of the group in question is unclear or mixed it must be male, "Anyone may have his money back" or "Someone left his pen here." In this linguistic system, women become invisible. Clearly, language shapes the mind: If it's not in the language, it's not in the mind. What that says about the importance of women to society, however, is clear: They are simply not seen. What we see creates perception, signals the very importance of a thing.

The book of Genesis reads, as does every scripture of every religion on earth, about male/female dual creation out of the same substance: "Let us make humans in our own image, in our own image let us make them; male and female let us make them" (Genesis 1:26–27)—that is, God is male and female, not male. The scriptures reflect the reality of it, and the meaning is clear: the way we see God determines the way we see ourselves. The language we use shapes public perceptions about God. If we see God only as maleness, maleness becomes more Godlike than femaleness. Maleness becomes the nature of God and the norm of humankind, rather than simply one of its manifestations. If we limit ourselves to the Divine Masculine, we will never see the Divine Feminine.

The great figures of early Christianity centuries ago—Origen, Irenaeus, Anselm, Bernard of Clairvaux and Aelred—believed that the womb of God is the Divine Feminine, and that without that awareness of the motherhood of God, as well as the fatherhood of creation, we will never know the fullness of God in our own lives. None of us, neither women nor men. In the end the real depth of the spiritual life, the real development of the psychological, emotional life, depends on whether or not we each nourish the feminine image of God in us and around us as well as we do the image of the fatherhood of God. When churches refuse the language of the feminine dimension of God, when they delete female pronouns and so collapse the male and the female into "all men" and "dear brothers," and "God, our mother," into "God, the father," they deprive us of the whole spirit of God.

But as obvious as the problem may seem, it is every bit as much denied as it is affirmed by traditions that refuse the spiritual insights, the religious leadership of women, who subordinate women to the male masters (their local gods) who have beaten, burned, killed women around the globe, male masters whose religions justify it, who counsel women into servitude but never into leadership. The full stature of women is every bit as much suppressed by a church's or a religion's absence of emphasis on their moral wholeness—absence from moral and theological decision-making—as it is enshrined by their empty insistence on the spiritual value of women. Although theological development omits women, the theological situation is clear: Everything written about us is without us! So we limp through life one-sided, empty-hearted, underdeveloped. We become spiritual amnesiacs, spiritual orphans, spiritual cyclops with a very myopic view of God and other religions, too. It blinds us— even women ourselves—to our moral agency, our responsibility, our leadership gifts.

Where does this notion of the Divine Feminine come from? Is the question of the Divine Feminine simply a current fad? A silly notion of even sillier feminists? Or could it possibly have deep and ineradicable roots in the tradition itself? However much we mock the idea, the truth is ironically that every major spiritual tradition on earth carries within it, at its very center, in its ancient core, an awareness of the Divine Feminine. In Hinduism, Shakti—the great mother, the feminine principle—is seen as the sum total of all the life-giving energy of the universe. She is the source of all. In Buddhism, Tara is seen as the perfection of wisdom, and, in Buddhism, wisdom is life's highest metaphysical principle! Tara is considered the light and the prime source of Buddhahood and so of all Buddhas to follow.

And in the Hebrew scriptures—the ground of the entire Abrahamic family (Jewish, Christian and Muslim)—the God to whom Moses says, "Who shall I say sent me?" answers not, "I am he who am"; not "I am she who am"; but, "I am who am." I am Being! I am the essence of all life; I am the spirit that breathes in everyone, the source that magnetizes every soul. I am the one in whose image all human beings, male and female, Genesis says clearly, are made. "I am" is, in other words, ungendered, unsexed, pure spirit, pure energy, pure life. That assurance we have, note well, on God's own word: "I am who am." Let there be no mistake about it: woman or man, man or woman—the full image of God is in you: masculine and feminine, feminine and masculine godness. Hebrew scripture is clear, and the Christian and Islamic scriptures, as well. God is neither male nor female—God is of the essence of both and both are of the essence of God.

Actually, lest we be fooled by our own patriarchal inclinations to make God in our own small, puny, partial male images, the Hebrew scriptures are full of the female attributes of God. In Isaiah (42:14) the Godhead "cries out as a woman in labor." To the psalmist, God is a nursing woman on whose breast the psalmist leans "content as a child that has been weaned" (Psalm 131:2). In Hosea (11:3–4) God claims to be a cuddling mother who takes Israel in her arms. In Genesis (3:21) God is a seamstress who makes clothes out of skins for both Adam and Eve. And in Proverbs, God-she, wisdom, Sophia, "raises her voice in the streets," "is there with God 'in the beginning'" (8:22–31), "is the homemaker who welcomes the world to her table" (9:5), shouting as she does, "Enter here! Eat my food, drink my wine."

After centuries of suppressing the female imagery and the feminine attributes given in scripture in order to establish the patriarchy of lords and kings and priests and popes and power-brokers as the last word and only word of every failing institution in humankind—no wonder we are confused about who God is. But God is not! Scripture is clear: God does not have—and clearly never has had—an identity problem. Our images of God must be inclusive because God is not mother, no, but God is not father either. God is neither male nor female. God is pure spirit, pure being, pure life—both of them. Male and female, in us all.

What signs do we have, then, of the authentic role of the feminine in the spiritual life? Who are the women that God has raised up in the Jewish, Christian and Islamic scriptures to show us the spiritual power, the leadership roles and the qualities of women alive and working in the economy of salvation and what do they say to us today? Moses' mother had an intuition that no woman could see the face of the oppressed and oppress it. So, with great faith and keen insight she set her condemned Jewish infant where the daughter of the Egyptian king herself would find this doomed child. Together two women—one Jewess, one Arab—joined hands across their differences to subvert the enemy system that male power and an irrational kind of reason had devised. Because of feminine intuition and passion for life, an entire people was saved. It is, too, the midwives Shiphrah and Puah who refuse to destroy Jewish newborns and save the children of Israel.

Queen Esther was a woman God lifted up to model the power of feminine strength. Esther is scripture's "well-placed woman." Esther, the Jewess, has after all—on account of her beauty, of course—been taken by the Assyrian king from the Jewish ghetto to the palace harem. As a result, Esther is the one safe Jew in the kingdom. She is respected and established. But Esther is a "lady." She knows her place in a world where self-development is a male prerogative and male protection is a woman's only defense. But Esther, under the impulse of the Divine Feminine, is willing to sacrifice it all—her position, her security, her very life—for the sake of her people. "Though no one may go to the King without being called," under threat of death, "I will go to the King to plead for the people," Esther says, "whether he calls me or not. And if I perish, I perish." On her account, the people survived and thrived. Surely this world needs the leadership of Divine Feminine feeling for victims of unbridled power now. When men are trained simply to take orders without question. When the best men rock no boats, call no consciences, critique no systems—civil or ecclesiastical—for fear of falling off the corporate or ecclesiastical ladder, someone must be willing to die for the truths of equality and difference.

Sarah, the woman of God, was open to the possibility that what the world called "rational" was not the only possible approach to a problem. "Sarah will conceive in her old age," the angel told Abraham, "and bear a son." The scripture says, "Sarah laughed." But I don't think Sarah laughed. I think Sarah hooted. Nice boys, these angels, but not too smart. She was, after all, way past menopause. Way past child-bearing age. Way past the very thought of pregnancy. And she told the angel so. But when the impossible happened she was open to it. She didn't reject it; she didn't set out to wrench the world to her own design. She accepted her role in this new world and she led the way for others. "Receptivity is the quality," the American Pulitzer Prize-winning poet Mark Van Doren says, that "takes ideas in and treats them royally, on the grounds that someday one of them may be king." Thanks to the receptivity of Sarah to a new idea of life and her new role in it, a whole people was raised up.

Clearly, women have been an essential part of God's economy of salvation from its foundation in religions in both West and East. What does all of this have to do with women of spirit and faith here and now? Why should we even consider the subject of the Divine Feminine at all? In the light of scripture's own images of God, in every religion everywhere, what kind of a life-denying, God-diminishing question is it to ask whether there is such a thing as a feminine dimension to God? On what grounds, then, can we possibly deny the feminine face of God among us an equal place at every table: corporate boards, decision-making synods, ecclesiastical councils, Qur'anic academies and sharia judgeships? How can women be denied the chance to be listened to, the right perhaps even to be heard, the fullness of moral agency and a public role to be reckoned with?

The social implications of ignoring or denying a topic such as this are enormous, life-changing, spiritually stunting. By casting God in human form, in one human form only, we limit our knowledge of God. We ignore the feminine dimension of God in the world and God in women as well. We leave life to the warriors, rather than to wisdom figures. We make masculinity the divine norm, ignoring and devaluing the feminine part of ourselves, in both women and men. We enthrone maleness, masculinity, the macho. God the father, God the avenging judge, God the warrior, God the lawgiver and God the perfectionist overwhelm the fullness of the image of God for us. We create a distant and unemotional God that comes with the image of an exclusively masculine God—all rational and all powerful—that affects our life at every stage and every moment. The model we have been given of the all-male God exercises power over everything, so we get confused trying to explain God's failure to use his power in order to save us from dangers.

Without a conscious awareness of the rest of the essence of God, of the Divine Feminine in God, we lose sight of God our mother, who forms us and influences us and encourages us to do good—not to be perfect but to do our best. We fail to remember God the mother who encourages us to repent and repair our mistakes, misjudgments, immaturities, God the mother who enables us to survive them. To understand God as Divine Feminine is to realize that all creation is co-creation. That creation is at least as much about what we do with creation to complete it, lead it to new life once we have it, as it is about the notion that it was given to us in a fixed form. God, for instance, did not create nuclear bombs—humans did—and we can uncreate them anytime we want to, provided someone exercises leadership of the Divine Feminine to show us the way. The common response to attempts to reduce nuclear weapons is always seen as a loss of total power—the one attribute that is God's alone. Instead we pray for peace, but do little or nothing to press politicians to practice it!

We must realize that God is the mother who carries us rather than lords it over us, who leads us to face the fact that the fate of the earth is largely in our hands. The God who is both feminine and masculine energy, the God who in ourselves we all image—more of this or less of that—both feminine and masculine in each of us, not only raises standards for us to meet but helps us over the bar. This God—this Divine Mother God—feels compassion for us, as scripture says so clearly, "I have heard the cry of my people" (Exodus 3:7). This Mother God feels anger and pain when we suffer: "I am sending you to deliver them" (Exodus 3:10). This Mother God in us feels care and concern when we struggle: "Be not afraid, Abram, I am your shield" (Genesis 15:1). It is this God and we who go on now creating the world together, feeling together its pain, working together to re-create it. Leading other men and women to do the same.

This God is not only the Divine Masculine, medieval lord and master, father, warrior and judge. This God is also the Divine Feminine—the one who feels, the one who cares as well as prescribes, the one who is nursing mother as well as protective father. The one who is also Divine and Feminine. This is the God who is completely other—and completely like us at the same time—in affection and care, in feeling and hope. This is the God who brings the world together—Hindu, Buddhist, Jewish, Christian and Muslim—listening, learning, loving the other. If God is all being, all there is, masculine and feminine, then Plato's God of total power, total distance, total indifference, and total emotional detachment is deficient. A God like that lacks love, lacks the will to be co-creative in a co-creative world. A God like that lacks the compassion and the empathy it takes to love the imperfect perfectly well. That male God is the one we have fashioned at our peril. By ignoring the value of the feminine, we have made for ourselves a patriarchal God for a world in which feeling is the necessary glue that holds that world together. We have made for ourselves a God to keep everybody else under control.

It is in the name of the God made male that women have been suppressed and ignored and reviled, called lesser, called inferior, called irrational in every male-controlled religion. Why doesn't God fix such an obvious injustice? Because God didn't make the situation; humans did. It is humans who warp the theology, humans who ignore the scriptures, humans who create a world designed to make the powerful more powerful and to divinize themselves at the expense of every other religion on earth. It is humans who fail to lead us to a fuller image of God. Humans, to be true to their own image of God, must now undo that imbalance—for the sake of the entire world, for the humanity of women and for authenticity of religion. No, God does not "fix" the world for us. But awareness of the fullness of God is the reality that requires us to fix it. God Divine Mother and God Divine Father is exactly what demands that being in all its glory—black and white, gay and straight, female and male—be respected and revered and embraced. Until all are, the fullness of the life that is God is only half alive in us, no matter how profusely we proclaim our rationality, no matter how confidently we argue our righteousness, no matter how sincerely we exalt our religiosity.

As it stands, we have enthroned the image of God the father. We have abandoned the image of God the mother, and as a result women, one way or the other, have become the invisible majority of the human race. By virtue of being female and in the name of God and religion, women the world over are kept out of social systems, out of schools and social status, out of work and financial security, out of property and politics, out of literacy and life support, out of food and water—even out of the pronouns of the language they dare to speak. Not because they are poor, but solely because they are women. Indeed, once we make God male, only males are really visible, only males are really the norm, the crown of creation—especially in our churches! Even there we call God Rock of Ages, Door of Heaven, Key of David, Dove of Peace, Tree of Life, Father of the Universe—but never, ever Mother. What can that possibly be but blatant sexism as well as bad philosophy, deficient theology, and an edited version of the scriptures? How can that not distort our very notion of leadership? After all, the scriptures demonstrate for us the essential role and the central place of the feminine, not a glorification of the female in the design of God.

Process philosophers say that feeling is a characteristic of the Divine Feminine. But the male world also says that it is feeling that really enfeebles a woman. High Vatican officials, for instance, issued documents a few years ago warning the church about the presence of women on marriage tribunals: "Their tender hearts render them unable to make right judgments." Feelings corrode the brain, in other words. Feelings weaken the will, they say. Feelings obscure the truth, they say. While the male world leads us to weapons of mass destruction, the will to ruthless power and lies about male superiority, they tell us that feelings diminish our effectiveness! Tell that to the woman who washed the feet of Jesus with her tears and dried them with her hair. Tell that to the Marys who, frightened, nevertheless followed Jesus all the way to the cross. Tell that to the women who went weeping to the tomb. Who even remembers and above all, who cares, about all the "reasonable" men who were not with them there where all the world has since wanted to be?

Tell the women philanthropists who, Luke says, "supported him out of their own substance," who recognized Jesus for the rest of us and made his work possible. No women—no Jesus! Tell women that feeling is their downfall and our bane. Tell them that feeling is the disease that renders women unfit to lead, to hold authority, to make decisions.

You see, it is not what sexism says about women that is sinful. It is what sexism says about God that is heresy, that corrupts the spirit. Doesn't sexism really imply that God is all powerful—

except when it comes to women, at which point the God who could draw water from a rock and raise the dead to life is totally powerless to work as fully through a woman as through a man? Is this the same God who also said: "Let us make humans in our own image: female and male let us make them"?

What will women bring to churches in crisis and a planet in peril? What will women bring to the spirit of the times? Woman will bring womanhood, that's what, to where only male lordship has been permitted to lead—distant, indifferent and dictatorial. It is womanliness that is the invisible gift, the unseen presence, the continuing reminder of the Divine Feminine in and over all of humankind. Woman must bring to leadership—the missing dimension of the God-life in us all—enabling it in men and fulfilling it in women; the missing link of a theology everywhere, in every tradition, not only our own, that understands the nature of God but has yet to make it real so that we can all become what we are meant to become. So that we demonstrate, rather than simply profess, our respect for women, and women's insights, and women's values and women's experiences. So that the women of our time everywhere may make the fullness of the love of God real for us all. Then we may all come to know ourselves, to be in the womb of our mother God. And right the images of God in every religion everywhere.

No doubt about it, women leaders like Miriam, prophetesses like Huldah, judges like Deborah, liberators like Judith, keepers of the line of David like Naomi and Ruth, the women at Jesus' tomb—all of them break through the patriarchal world of Hebrew scripture with earth-shaking regularity and clear recollection of the other face of God's presence and power. In a world in which one-third live in abject poverty, two-thirds of those are women and girls—the poorest, hungriest, most venerable, most threatened, least cared for, least listened to population in the world—patience is not enough. We need the courage now to lead us to a consciousness of the Divine Feminine in ways that make life changes for the world, for women in every religion everywhere. And, that will, at the same time, enrich the emotional, spiritual development of men.

The Talmud reads, "If we had been holier people, we would have been angrier oftener." May God give us all the grace to feel a life-giving burst of holy anger!

8.

The Woman Who Wouldn't

When Vision Gives Voice to Dissent

In October 2012, Hildegard of Bingen, almost a thousand years after her birth, will finally have been elevated to the status of doctor of the church. And yet, until Pope Benedict XVI proclaimed her a saint by fiat, Hildegard was never canonized despite the fact that the process was begun fifty-four years after her death. In 1979, when the German bishops petitioned Rome for a second time to make her a doctor of the church, that petition, too, was overlooked. Thérèse of Lisieux, "The Little Flower," was chosen instead. The question is, What was there about this woman that took so long for such official recognition? And why did this name never really die in the memory of the universal church? And what can she possibly mean to us in this day and age?

This is the story of a great woman: a mystic, a visionary, a reformer—a dissenter.

"Dissent" is one of the more difficult dimensions of public discourse to define. It's not the same as the political sparring that is expected of political parties—even required at some level—if a republic is to be a republic. And yet, dissent is easy to recognize.

Dissent comes out of the depth of the heart and exists only in service to what both sides say they are each committed to preserving.

It comes out of a soul in anguish over life that must be bartered in the process of saving it.

Most of all, dissent always has a place and a time and a face we do not expect to see in this place at this time. It has the character of exactly what the institution wants most to produce: total loyalty and complete identification. The problem is that both sides define their one same loyalty differently. The establishment is always loyal to the very institutionalism of the institution in question. The dissenter is always most loyal instead to what the institution itself claims to be about.

As a result, loneliness is at the very heart of dissent. Loneliness is its character and isolation is its cost: It is one young man facing a row of tanks in Tiananmen Square. It is the pacifist Dorothy Day on a hunger strike in a Washington jail for having the temerity to protest in behalf of woman's suffrage at the gates of the White House. It is the African American Rosa Parks refusing to get out of her seat on a public bus. It is the few who hold out against total dissolution of the highest ideals of any institution.

In which case, Hildegard of Bingen is indeed a dissenter.

A Culture in Turmoil

The Europe into which Hildegard had been born fairly exploded with new life. It was an era of intellectual revival and international commerce. Vernacular literatures were emerging. Seafaring navigation equipment made exploration, trade and human contact possible. Medieval universities made the spread of Arabic learning, Greek and Roman classics, and modern ideas possible. Failed Crusades weakened both church and crown. And at the same time, the rise of scholasticism brought a new kind of learning that recognized the use of secular learning, reason and logic as handmaids of the faith. It was a period of great tension, an unstable and feuding papacy, changing ideas, contrary theologies and highly impacting people—Bernard of Clairvaux, Anselm of Canterbury, and Peter Damian, among others—all bent on reforming a church mired in corruption. It was a world rife with lax clergy and simmering with new ideas. It was, in other words, an era very much like our own.

And there, into the midst of it, came Hildegard of Bingen, one of the brightest of them all. The scene had the energy of a shooting star, on one hand, and signaled a world ripe for dissent on the other. "The Vita of Hildegard" hints of it: "In the eleven hundredth year after the Incarnation of Christ, the teaching and fiery justice of the Apostles, which Christ had established among the Christians and spiritual people, began to slow down and turn into hesitation. I was born in those times."

Born in 1098, Hildegard was the tenth child of minor nobility in Bermersheim, Germany, yes. But in 1106, she was given to the church at the age of eight in gratitude for God's blessings to the rest of the family. It was a time-honored practice, one that became for her, however, a life commitment with an unlikely twist.

For most people, life is a kind of scavenger hunt. We move from one part of it to another looking for small, obscure objects along the way that can enable us to make the best of the helter-skelter world in which we live. Sometimes, though, as in Hildegard's case, life comes to us rather than our having to find it ourselves one uncertain, often painful, new step at a time. In that case, what can we possibly do? Our direction has been set for us already. A template into which we are meant to step, quietly and with predictable docility. The questions then are clear ones: Do we simply go along, passive participants in our own lives? Or are we left to carve our uniqueness out of it ourselves, one routine decision at a time?

One thing for certain: Seventy-three years of life in a convent would not seem to be the place either to plunge through life with limitless zest, choosing this, discarding that, or to choose a life famous for its regularity and then pursue it irregularly. But as a matter of fact, for Hildegard it was. She made it so.

For Hildegard, as a woman, convent life was life changing. Her major dissent, it could even be said, is that she dared to be herself in such an age and place at all. As a result, for other women she has become a life-changing model of a different way to be.

A Life of Reflection

The historical skeleton of her life is ostensibly a simple one. At the age of eight she was entrusted to the spiritual tutelage of Jutta, an anchoress attached to the male Benedictine monastery of Disibodenberg. By the time Jutta died in 1136, some thirty years later, Hildegard, after years of instruction in monastic life, became the magister or prioress of the little group.

Perhaps even more important, in that period, Hildegard "instructed by the Living Light, put her hand to writing" and began the first of her great works, *Scivias—To Know the Ways of God*. A major theological dissertation on the spiritual life, it would have been a classic under any conditions. But this was a theological study of all the major topics of Christianity—and it was written by a woman. It was a major display of deep spiritual reflection, of intellectual independence and personal spiritual development. Clearly, the dissent had already begun.

A Struggle to Become Independent

By 1147, furthermore, the number of her disciples had grown. The living conditions at the male monastery became more and more inadequate for so large a group of women. The abbess Hildegard, then forty-nine years old, followed her vision and left the confines of Disibodenberg to set up her own independent women's community. She moved the then-eighteen members of the community and their dowries into the new monastery which she herself had designed, this time with running water and ample facilities. And despite the disapproval of the abbot.

The loss of the public attention and gifts which Hildegard's work and presence brought to Disibodenberg surely gave the abbot pause. But the loss of the women's dowries and the financial well-being they signaled for the abbey made the move totally unacceptable. Abbot Kuno's demands, entreaties, and castigations counted for nothing. Hildegard would not return to Disibodenberg. Instead, she opened her own monastery in Rupertsberg and wrote back to him, "And you, O man, who have been placed as a visible shepherd, rise up and hasten quickly to justice, so that you will not be criticized by the great doctor for not having cleansed your flock from dirt, for not having anointed them with oil."

Clearly, Disibodenberg was not a good place for women. But to leave it without the abbot's consent asserted the kind of independence unheard of in women in that era.

More than that, once settled in her new community in Rupertsberg, Hildegard prevailed on the archbishop of Mainz to confirm the act. Then, she also prevailed on Emperor Frederick Barbarossa, whom she had also upbraided—in one instance, it appears, for dismissing an archbishop friend of hers and in another for supporting a rival pope during one of the frequent papal schisms of the time. Barbarossa went so far as to commit to a secret document in which he promised his full protection in the event that anyone—anyone at all in either church or crown—attempt to suppress it. The boldness of it all simply takes the breath away.

And yet, the bare bones of Hildegard's monastic life do not begin to describe the scope and depth of her dissent.

No doubt about it: Hildegard, the woman, had a sense of herself and her own moral agency that women in the twentieth century are still in the process of learning. She knew herself to be an intelligent human being. She made major personal and social decisions, not only beyond the limits set for women in her time but even in the face of male disapproval. She simply refused to live within norms that made her less than the creature of God she knew herself to be.

A dissenter? Indeed. In full bloom.

A Woman with a Mind of Her Own

She was a thinker—both theologian and ethicist, in fact. Her major books, *Scivias* and *The Book of the Rewards of Life,* defined the entire spiritual life when her world could not imagine women moralists and her church definitely did not want women theologians.

She was a woman who operated under what she knew to be the impulse of the God within. She had lived in a world of inner visions since the age of six and grew more and more in tune with them as she grew. She wrote:

> When I was forty-two years and seven months old, a burn-
> ing light of tremendous brightness coming from heaven
> poured into my entire mind. . . . All of a sudden, I was able
> to taste of the understanding of the narration of books. I
> saw the psalter clearly and the evangelists and other Catho-
> lic books of the Old and New Testament.

Clearly, her visions were not sensual. Her visions were intellectual. She did not "see"; she simply "knew." She intuited; she did not "hear." She goes on:

> The visions which I saw I did not perceive in dreams nor
> when asleep nor in a delirium nor with the eyes or ears of
> the body. I received them when I was awake and looking

around with a clear mind, with the inner eyes and ears, in open places according to the will of God.

Led by those internal insights, prodded by that sense of the will of God, Hildegard became the feminine voice of God for women—"God's little trumpet," she called herself. She was a fully functioning moral agent, a model of female agency when women were considered the dependents of men, more children than adults, the lesser of two orders of human beings who did not have either the credentials or the capacity to be full adults.

A Scholarly and Independent Intellectual Life

The very scope and volume of her work were overwhelming. She was an intellectual, a composer, an encyclopedist, who wrote the only two medical texts produced in twelfth-century Germany. She was a scientist who understood ecology and sustainability and the "web of creation" and the life of the universe before ecology was a word and despite the theology of domination that had become the clarion cry of a patriarchal worldview. She was the dissenting feminine voice of God in a world that defined men, the males of the species, as agents of God free to control, horde, consume and destroy the natural resources of the human race. Hildegard's theology of *viriditas*—of the greening power and purpose of all life—redefined what it means to be "reasonable" in the face of a rationality now defined as dominion without limits and control without benefit of compassion.

Greater intellectual dissent than hers at that time is difficult to imagine.

She was a visionary, a mystic, a justice seeker, a Benedictine woman steeped in the psalms and the scriptures who saw life through the eye of God and named injustice, indifference and corruption wherever she found it. She chastised both popes and kings, priests and emperors to right a world rife with Crusades, ecclesiastical corruption and civil carnage.

At the age of sixty she began four speaking tours of the Rhine, speaking from castles and cathedrals about the sins and errors of the time, regardless whose. She was a prolific writer who not only called sin wherever she saw it but raised the best of Christian ideals in everything she did, for everyone to see. A "prophet" they called her as she called for the reform of the church and honesty in high places.

She wrote about the priests of the time:

But because they have the power of preaching, imposing penance, and granting absolution, for that reason, they hold us in their grasp like ferocious beasts. Their crimes fall upon us and through them the whole church withers, because they do not proclaim what is just; and they destroy the law in their drunkenness and they commit copious adulteries, and because of such sins, they judge us without mercy. For they are also plunderers of their congregations, through their avarice, devouring whatever they can; and with their offices they reduce us to poverty and indigence, contaminating both themselves and us. For this reason, let us judge and single them out in a fair trial for they lead us astray.

She wrote to Pope Anastasius IV:

So it is, O man, that you who sit in the chief seat of the Lord, hold him in contempt when you embrace evil, since you do not reject it but kiss it, by silently tolerating it in depraved men.

And though she revered Bernard of Clairvaux, whose words inspirited the misbegotten Crusades, she spoke out against the participation of the clergy in the militarism of knighthood:

> How can it be right that the shaven-headed with their robes and chasubles should have more soldiers and more weapons than we do? Surely, too, it is inappropriate for a cleric to be a soldier and a soldier a cleric?

The system simply could not break her. Justice was her passion, her impulse. Her writings reek with it and her life was exhausted in its service.

Right to the end, she strove against the clergy of the area because of what she saw as an unjust demand. Ordered to remove from the community cemetery the body of a man whom the local bishop had excommunicated, she refused. In fact, in order to protect the corpse from abuse, Hildegard herself at the age of eighty walked among the headstones using her cane to destroy all sign of the man's fresh grave and marking so it could not possibly be moved.

She wrote of that situation:

> I saw in my soul that if we followed their command and exposed the corpse, such an expulsion would threaten our home with great danger, like a vast blackness—It would envelop us like a dark cloud that looms before tempests and thunderstorms. . . . So we did not dare expose him . . . lest we seem to injure Christ's sacraments.

They punished her for that by putting the entire community under interdict that denied this community the right to have Mass, receive communion or sing the Divine Office, a deprivation that would wound the soul of any Benedictine community of women to this day. They tried to starve her spiritually, to reject her totally. And still Hildegard and her community would not relent in their commitment to the Law above the law.

The Sanctity of Struggle and Sign of the Times

Within months of this last great struggle for justice and compassion, Hildegard died, unbeaten and unbroken. Why? Because as a Benedictine woman, steeped in the scriptures every day of her life, she could not, with integrity, do less.

Surely this great Benedictine woman is a woman for our own times, one who knows sexism and decries it, knows militarism and deplores it, knows clericalism and rejects it, knows corruption and unmasks it, knows faith and puts the gospel above the institution.

Hildegard, a dissenter of the first class, is, the Vatican itself assures us, a blazing sign of spiritual brilliance for us all. Even here. Even now.

In her own time, Bernard of Clairvaux himself begged Pope Eugenius "not to allow such a brilliant light to be covered by silence." Now, in this century, in our time, this silence is finally officially broken.

The only question now is whether or not we will do the same.

PART II

SEEDS OF A NEW SPIRITUALITY

Introduction

The question, What will you do? is at the core of spiritual maturity, of spiritual commitment.

—Joan Chittister

As she signals the ever-growing need for conversion to a discipleship marked by maturity, so does Sister Joan persist in her emphasis on the centrality of ongoing spiritual maturity. To her, they are of a piece.

The mature disciple is committed to spiritual growth and understands such commitment is lifelong. Sister Joan's passionate focus over decades has encouraged a spirituality that is prophetic for, as she has written, "The prophet knows that pious practices can easily become a substitute for religion."

What is the foundation for such moral and spiritual maturity? Her answer is fourfold: to become conscious of God's presence everywhere; to behold the sacredness of all life; to listen attentively to the ever present voice of the Spirit; and to humbly embrace our place in this universe. Such are the keys to developing one's authentic humanity, as well as one's appreciation for beauty and the artists who create it.

Further, with her inimitable voice, Sister Joan reminds her readers that "it is precisely our idea of God that is the measure of our spiritual maturity"—a wake-up call every serious seeker should heed.

Whether being "a voice for the voiceless" poor and oppressed in Latin America, confronting the challenges women religious faced and continue to face after Vatican II, extolling the forgotten but no less potential values of fasting in this day and age, seeding new life on this planet rather than its destruction, Sister Joan urges immersion in the dire challenges of our age. She beckons us to embrace a spiritual journey beyond mere compliance, through awareness and into transformation. Then, and only then, will the seeker begin to see the world as God sees the world; then, and only then, will the seeker begin to weave with grace a truly human life, marked by moral and spiritual maturity. Such is the fruit of a lifelong commitment to daily ongoing conversion of mind, heart and action.

—*Mary Hembrow Snyder*

9.

The Burden of Nonviolence

A Jewish tale relates that a young woman once said to an old woman, "Old woman, what is life's heaviest burden?" And, we are told, the old woman replied, "Life's heaviest burden is to have no burden to carry at all."

Ah, yes, the message is clear: The smallest of us is each responsible for something bigger than ourselves. To do less is to be less than we should be. The problem is that it is often so difficult to know exactly what the big thing really is. Martha of Bethany got her responsibilities wrong for a while, we know. Judas couldn't get them straightened out at all. The fishing disciples were sure, at first, that fishing was far more important than following Jesus. We need not, in other words, smugly conclude that we in our time will know our responsibilities when we see them.

It never crossed my mind when I was growing up, for instance, that a Christian's real responsibility was not to the church but to the gospel, not to the country, but to the world, not just to my own kind but to everyone, not simply to the private things that I wanted to do but to the great things that had to be done whether I wanted to do them or not.

And the struggle for insight is not getting much easier as life goes along. The only difference is that now at least I know that there are questions. For instance, there are faults in the church, but is risking disunity by pointing them out necessarily a better state of affairs? There are major policy mistakes in the country, but as people in the peace movement are so often told these days, is the danger of finding ourselves in an even worse system a better solution than simply bearing the little sin of nuclear possibility? There are sick and old and poor and wounded in my own society, but knowing that I really can do very little about all of that, isn't it just as well to leave those things to the officials whose responsibility it is to respond rather than to do so little noisily?

The questions were all bad enough as they were until fifteen of my own sisters in my own monastery gathered to begin the study of the Pax Christi vow of nonviolence with a view to pronouncing it in the priory chapel on the anniversary of the bombing of Hiroshima. Then the clanging really started in my head. Of what good are foolishness and symbol in life? Of what good is a drop in the bucket? Of what use is it for the weak to institutionalize their weakness? Let's get excited when George Shultz or Zbigniew Brzezinski or Ronald Reagan take a vow of nonviolence, not when it's fifteen nuns, fifteen peaceniks, fifteen women. Let's hear it from the men before we think it means anything.

And then I began to think of the old woman's warning that to have nothing to carry at all was a greater burden than carrying what was too heavy for you.

It is an irreparable burden to be without conscience. To live at a moment of time when my country is capable of annihilating the planet and make no attempt to say no is to be weighed down in soul. What kind of hollowness does it take to see the effects of sin but have no sense of sin?

It is an irreparable burden to be without voice. The closest thing I know to the burden of silence in the face of the sacrilege of militarism and macho and nuclear madness is not that it makes a person a sheep; it is the pain of not being able to scream in the middle of a nightmare.

It is a galling burden to be without obligation. Life becomes perfectly meaningless when we are finally convinced that nothing we do has any meaning. Why then do we live at all? Leo Rosten wrote once: "The purpose of life is not to be happy; the purpose of life is to matter—to have it make a difference that you lived at all." If I am not obliged to something bigger than myself, even though it may be unattainable, then has my life really been worth anything at all?

It is a frightening burden to be without trust. To live in a nuclear world and never say a word against it is to live in a bubble of arrogance and hate. And arrogance and hate are the worst kind of pollution. Arrogance poisons reality and hate poisons life. Arrogance and hate make diplomacy and negotiation and human community impossible because they render trust important. Someone has to be able to be humble enough not to have to be the best, the first, the perfect. Someone has to be trusting enough to say, "I believe; I accept; I'll try." That is, perhaps, Gideon's best gift to the church. Having raised an army of forty thousand to do battle for his God, Gideon was instructed to reduce the army to three hundred and face the enemy with screeching trumpets and banging lanterns so that when the battle was over its observers would not say, "See what Gideon has done for God," but "See what God has done for Gideon."

Indeed, my fifteen sisters have confronted me with the real burden of my life.

The real burden of my life is not nuclear disarmament and elimination of sexism. The real burden of my life is the vow of nonviolence. The real burden of my life is the thought of being without conscience, without voice, without a sense of obligation, without the strong defense of trust.

Oh, true, the vow will not be easy. It means I must be a peaceful peacemaker. It means I must turn every moment of ridicule into resurrection. It means I must learn to love what does not love me. It means that I must make a clear distinction between being assertive and being aggressive. It means that, like Gideon, I must go forth without an army in a culture where John Wayne is king, Rambo is Mister Everyman, and Al Capone got respect.

And will it work? Well, it worked in India for Gandhi. It worked in Selma for Martin Luther King. It worked in the Philippines for Cory Aquino. And it worked for the third graders of St. Veronica's School when I went there as a child. Every year we all got up in church and recited the Pledge of the Legion of Decency, promising that we wouldn't go to sleazy movies even if it meant we would never see another film on Saturday afternoons in our entire lives. And it affected the film industry: they had to categorize their films and they had to provide what we wanted or face ignominious defeat at the hands of the third graders of the world. I trust that it can work again.

Imagine a world whose third graders and ushers and teachers and fathers and college jocks vowed never to use violence again to achieve their ends. Vowed not that they would be passive, just that they would be nonviolent. Imagine the strength of the challenge.

Well, sixteen of us are going to start, without waiting for Shultz and Brzezinski and Reagan.

Perhaps I'm wrong. Perhaps it won't be effective at all. But the old woman has taught me a lesson for life. For me, at least, it is better to bear the burden of being ineffective than it is to bear the burden of being unconscionable.

10.

The Place of Prophecy in Dark Times

The Light That Does Not Dim

Robert Louis Stevenson told a story of growing up in Scotland around the turn of the century that says a great deal, I think, about the purpose of life. The Stevenson family, Robert recounted, lived on a hillside above a small town. As a boy, he watched every evening from the window above the square as the local lamplighter went through the town below lighting each of the village street lights. "Look, Mother, look," the boy said. "There is a man down there in the city who punches holes in the darkness." Nothing, I believe, says it better. The role of the prophet in society, if history is to be trusted at all, is to punch holes in the darkness of our souls.

In a society such as ours, however, the image of prophet abides uneasy in the public psyche, a foreigner from a faraway land, a dim memory from a time and place long gone and never really known. To mention prophets in the technological here-and-now conjures up notions of opening drum rolls and closing thunder cracks. Clearly, to the modern mind, prophecy is the stuff of mountains and deserts, not of cities and sophisticates. It is proper to the people of the Book, perhaps, but out of place in patriotic, church-going USA where God and country, altar and flag are all too often one and the same thing. It is certainly unwanted in a church where orthodoxy is more welcome than questions and criticism is read as infidelity.

Prophetic presence—the image of the scorching eye and the burning lips—is not a comfortable concept in a culture that conforms to business uniforms and corporate hierarchies, to male control of theological thought. The last thing in the world such a world can tolerate is a person with a soul of steel and a heart that does not conform quietly to customary corruptions and systemic sin, to public disregard of outcries against injustice and inequality in any place at any time, to control that calls itself tradition. On the contrary. This is a society where those who have the security that employment brings—and many do not—get on the highway for work by sunup and, by and large, settles in by sundown for the night, unaware of another world around them, or disinterested if they are aware. This is a society clearly more comfortable with the concepts of freedom and order than it is with social change and prophetic challenge. We accept political debate because that maintains the system. We rest most uneasy when the system itself is the question.

In a social climate such as this, the values taught to first graders and touted most highly throughout a person's entire life are independence and achievement, hard work and patriotism, institutionalism and relative prosperity. The goals we urge on generations to come presume, in fact, a very standard-brand existence. We want our children to get "ahead" in life, to become something and somebody, to know security and social acceptance, to be "nice." We encourage them to become stockbrokers and computer programmers, auto mechanics and armed services personnel. We do not, as a rule, press them to be social justice advocates, or feminist organizers or public defenders. The system is inherently just, we assume; women are naturally privileged, we argue; criminals—the accused—are guilty until proven innocent whatever the philosophical foundation of the justice system. In an environment that springs from such a system, a people are prepared to be steady and productive, not outraged and loud. People are expected to be "good," not necessarily to be courageous; the population is expected to be successful, not necessarily to be autonomous.

A culture of conformity is a predictable one indeed. It is built on achievement, on having it all, on making a good public appearance, on being religious models of religious establishments that support the government whatever it does. Its government talks about family values and leaves poor families without resources. Its churchgoers are careful to worship with the right people in the right places without questioning what the worship, worships. This society likes things to be smooth and comfortable, quick and easy, awarding and apolitical. The world and its problems become too big to bother about as individuals or too boring to contemplate next to MTV and ESPN. The great questions in life belong, in large part, to someone else—the government or the justice department, the military or the welfare office, the university or the chancery. The personal questions of life such a people handle in privacy. The show is the thing.

Most of all, a secularized society wants its religions—if religion is wanted at all—to be quiet and comforting. The civil religion, in a world where conformity and political chauvinism are key to social well-being, forms people for piety and dogma, for national virtues and institutional approval. Religion in such a system as this resides in the mind, not in the marketplace and certainly not to the detriment of the civic, economic and public values posited to be the core of the good life. The civil becomes the virtuous; the institutional norm becomes the measure of personal salvation.

Prophets, it would seem, are not cut out of such cultural cloth. Consequently, never has the prophetic dimension of religion been needed more. Never has the prophetic insight been more demanded by the times. Never has the nature of prophecy been more clouded.

The truth is that drum rolls and thunder cracks have little or nothing to do with the prophetic spirit. Prophets, in fact, have been quite ordinary people with souls attuned to ordinary insights. If truth were known, the more ordinary the prophet the more powerful the message, perhaps. The ordinary prophet calls into question the notion that the prophetic vocation is spiritually unique and requires us to come to see it as normal. As normal it is. The prophetic tradition to which we look for model and meaning is an assortment of simple people who found themselves in tension with what they knew in the center of their souls to be right and what they saw being institutional-ized around them. Isaiah, for instance, was a political adviser with the conscience of a flaming angel who wanted peace and refused to argue for war. Jeremiah was a priest who recognized the sins of his own nation and called for social conversion. Ezekiel was also a priest but an exile in Babylon, as well, who despite his years as a prisoner of war came to respect the humanity of his captors and called the rest of Israel to see them, too, as God's people. And this despite the orthodox position that being chosen by God meant that Israel alone was chosen.

Amos was a shepherd, a working man, who knew that the country was being built on the backs of the poor and said so. Micah was a simple man from a pathetic little village who stood up to the rich exploiters in the towns for their ruthless disre-gard of the commoners from the countryside and the laborers from the ghettoes. Political consultant, priest, farmer, small-town philosopher—all of them just like us. All of them in the system themselves. All of them apparently average citizens. Except for one thing: each of them listened to the voice of God within them. Each of them realized with urgency what the rest of us come to understand too slowly, perhaps, and often with pain, that God expects us to speak that Word. They failed to be seduced by religion itself.

They refused to believe that keeping the rules was the same as living the covenant. They knew a deeper spirituality. A voice within themselves called them to deeper truths than the sorry notion that salvation was achieved by Temple sacrifice. They knew that religion was not about the way a people went about ritual. Religion, they knew, was really meant to be about the way people go about life. They were prophets because they refused to separate the two. Religion, to the prophet, goes hand in hand with dailiness.

The prophet is the one in our midst who transcends religion for its own sake to become what real religion sets out to make us all—bearers of the heart of God to all the heartlessness of the world. Prophets speak aloud the voice of God we all hear within us but so successfully manage to stifle, compartmentalize, edit and ignore. The prophet is the one who speaks out of the contemplative heart. Prophecy is not religion in action; prophecy is contemplation in action. It is coming to proclaim aloud the God whom we know in silence. Prophecy lights up the sky with questions.

Prophecy comes as counterpoint to this culture. It demonstrates four approaches to the human enterprise, each of them contrary to the values of the system itself. Prophecy depends on autonomy rather than individualism; it requires a sense of community rather than independence; it gives a sense of the sacred to what would otherwise be mundane; it makes real religion out of right impulses which, under lesser conditions, might otherwise become mere piety. Contrary to superficial explanations of the phenomenon, prophecy is not magic, not fortune-telling, not extremism, not unorthodox. Prophecy is religion, that release of the Divine in the human, that calls the heart to reckless and righteous fullness of life in a world that puts premium on values that are only partially human, partly whole. Or, as La Roche-foucauld put it, "Those who live without folly are not so wise as they think."

The question is, then: What is the future of prophecy in a society such as ours? The answer depends, as it always has, on which is valued more as a person chooses one function from another: social capital, personal security or integrity of soul.

Autonomy and individualism, for instance, are not the same thing. The prophet chooses for an autonomy that brings to every human question a critical eye. Autonomy implies a freedom of soul that makes independent thinking possible. The prophetic heart is a heart free of the shackling that comes with the need for approval, that keeps us looking around the room to see whether or not people like what we are saying, that enables us to look at an issue and make a decision about it ourselves without having to have the permission of any institution to think it. The person who is autonomous is the person who, guided by principle and intent on the greatest good, thinks things through for themselves and gives other people the right to do the same.

Individualism, on the other hand, implies the process of self-expression, yes, but not necessarily the process of self-direction. There are individualists in every multitude who stand out in the gray crowd because they dye their hair purple or dance on tabletops in public or wear sweatshirts with clerical pants. But individualists, distinct as they may be, are often institution people, nevertheless. At the end of the day, they believe without question what the institution allows them to believe and climb its corporate ladders and salute its flags without a sound. And if they do not believe, they do not say what would jeopardize their right to be accepted as individualistic.

Autonomy dwarfs individualism by being larger than an individual can possibly be simply by virtue of being different. Autonomy of soul is what gives a person the courage it takes to stand alone, to measure the character of the institution against its constitutions, to critique the institution for the sake of the institution itself. As a result, autonomy is an institution's greatest protection and least valued gift. The social prophet is an autonomous person whose mind and heart and soul belong to no one but God.

Every day, however, autonomy becomes more and more threatening to systems which, in the face of great social ferment, fear the loss of control. The acceptance of the prophetic voice becomes less and less possible in institutions which are more dedicated to maintaining jurisdiction than they are to enabling the kind of vision it will take to move us beyond violence, beyond oppression, beyond hegemony to equality and justice, to the will of God for all humanity however oppressive the system may be, however the system claims its authority.

As autonomous as the prophet may be, however, prophecy to be real must embed itself in the needs of the community. Prophets do not seek their own agendas. They speak the mind of God for the needs of the least of the people. The public agitator who is not speaking for the poor and forgotten ones is not speaking in a prophetic tone of voice. Prophets speak for the poor. "And God said to Moses, 'I have observed the misery of my people who are in Egypt; I have heard their cry on account of their taskmasters. Indeed, I know their sufferings . . . and I have come down to deliver them. So come, I will send you to Pharaoh to bring my people, the Israelites, out of Egypt'" (Exodus 3:8–10). Where the protection of the poor is not the object of the proclamation, the speech is not prophetic. Clearly, prophecy in a country that elects people who promise to balance a military budget on the backs of the poor will not take kindly to a prophet's words. It is welfare for the rich that is promised here and now, not welfare for the poor.

Prophecy sees the sacred in the mundane. Sacrifice and piety, ritual and law are not its concerns, good as these may often be, unless and until these very elements become the stumbling blocks to the development of a mature spiritual life. Prophecy

weds the material to the spiritual, the wonders and wounds of
this world to what the prophets come to recognize as the will
of God for people. Prophecy, in other words, gives a sense of the
sacred to what the world dismisses as mundane, of no spiritual
account, as disposable items in the world's political repertoire.
It is the prophet who decries wars for oil, industrial slavery for
the living wage, the oppression of women in the name of the
natural law, the dismissal of the witness of Jesus in the light of
long-lived practices of the church. It is the prophet who finds
little welcome in the institutions of the time, political or ecclesiastical. The prophetic vocation, therefore, depends on people
who can live well on hope, trust in mercy and ask for little in
the way of public stamps of approval.

Prophecy makes real religion out of right impulses which,
under lesser conditions, might otherwise become mere piety. We
pray because we believe. We seek God because we believe that
God is. We search our souls for whispers of God there because
we know ourselves to be sparks of the Divine. We seek to follow God because we know that the mind of God, the Universal
Mind, the Living Heart of the Cosmos has created life, not to
taunt and tease and test and try us, but so that the goodness of
God might be reflected in us. To substitute the practices of the
faith for the meaning of the faith is religion's greatest sin. The
prophet knows that even the holy can become decadent, that
even the Temple can become corrupted, that even the church
can be reduced to Law when Love is what religion is really
about. The prophet knows that pious practices can easily become
a substitute for religion.

But the prophet raises our hearts and souls to the level of the
meaningful in life. Ritual makes us conscious of the sacred in
life; prophecy, the commitment to measure the world around us
according to the standards of the gospel, makes us its messengers. The prophet recalls the church to the terms of a covenant
that forbids the worship of false gods—money, power, sexism,

exclusivity. The prophets in society remind us as Amos did that oppression of the poor is wrong; as Hosea did that the church, too, can stray from its Center and collude with the powerful of the world; as Micah did that justice for the poor is essential to the salvation of the rich; as Isaiah did that militarism is sinful; as Jeremiah did that virtue is more important than orthodoxy; as Ezekiel did that God is in everyone everywhere and the rejection of anyone on the basis of race or gender is therefore wrong.

So what is the future of prophecy in our time in a society that is reactionary to the core and in a church that is more committed to maintaining its male self than in modeling the principles of justice and equality which it preaches to others? The future of prophecy in a society such as this is bare, bleak and lonely to be sure. At the same time, it is also glorious. In the end, surely the voice of truth will someday again, as it always, eventually, does, prevail over systems steeped in sin plain for the poor to see if only we ourselves refuse to mute the wails of a people in pain, of women in exile, of a world in poverty, of the little ones underfoot. "I have heard the cry of my people," Yahweh says. "I have seen their misery. And I mean to save them." The will of God for the poor endures. The only question now is the length of time it will take us to enflesh it in our own lives whatever the cost to ourselves.

There is no doubt that repression silences many—for a while. It is equally true that repression prepares the way for the ultimate undoing of the system. The Berlin Wall fell; the Soviet Union disintegrated; church resistance to the modern world ended "not with a bang but a whimper." Oh, yes. It is clearly kill-the-prophets time again, but the voice having once been heard, the message can never be forgotten; the vision having once been seen, the image can never be dimmed.

In a country that is dismantling its social welfare system, rejecting its poor, devoted in peacetime to wartime, and enslaving and endangering the globe, the voice of the prophet is strangely absent from the land. In a church that nurtures within itself the last official seed of sexism and a model of authoritarianism in a world bent on enfranchising the marginated, the prophet who holds the covenant as a mirror to the law is being cut down, silenced or banished from the center of the system.

But not to worry. Like Isaiah before them, the prophets of the day are standing outside the system training small bands to think like themselves so that when Yahweh's purge of a dying institution is complete, all over the world there will have been a series of small lights lit punching holes in the darkness around them.

11.

Oh, Wonder of Wonders

The Sufi tell stories that say all I think I'll ever know about finding God.

The first story is a disarming and compelling one. It is also, I think, a troublesome one, a fascinating one, a chastening one: "Help us to find God," the seeker begged the Elder. "No one can help you there," the Elder answered. "But why not?" the seeker insisted. "For the same reason that no one can help a fish to find the ocean." The answer is clear: There is no one who can help us find what we already have.

The second story is even more challenging. "Once upon a time," the Sufi say, "a seeker ran through the streets shouting over and over again, 'We must put God into our lives. We must put God into our lives.'" "Ah, poor soul," an Elder smiled wanly. "If only we realized the truth: God is always in our lives. The spiritual task is simply to recognize that."

As a Benedictine, a disciple of an order historically devoted to the Sacrament of the Ordinary, I know how disappointing, how exhilarating that kind of advice can be. The neophyte seeks to pass the test of spiritual heroics; the wise seek to accomplish only the testimony of integrity. The young think the task is to buy God by their good efforts; the insightful know that the task is to want God beyond the lure of lesser ends, including even the trappings of spirituality.

For my own part, I entered religious life intent on being spiritually intrepid. I wanted something far more romantic than the Sacrament of the Ordinary. I expected to find formulas tried and true, ideas that were esoteric, a life that was mystical, a regimen that was at least duly demanding, if not momentously ascetic. What I found were spiritual manuals that were convoluted and academic, at best, and a community that was simple and centered in God always. The writers had missed the mark; the women were living the life. It was very disappointing. And it was very right.

God is not in the whirlwind, not in blustering and show, scripture teaches us. God is in the breeze, in the very atmosphere around us, in the little things that shape our lives. God is in the contradictions that assail us, in the circumstances that challenge us, in the attitudes that impel us, in the motives that drive us, in the life goals that demonstrate our real aspirations, in the burdens that wear us down, in the actions that give witness to the values in our hearts. God is in the stuff of life, not in the airy-fairy of fertile imaginations bent on the pursuit of the preternatural. God is where we are, including in the very weaknesses that vie for our souls.

Benedictine spirituality attends to those things, not to tricks and trials designed to make spiritual athletes out of spiritual weaklings. Finding God depends on finding what determines our own lives and realizing in them the power and transcendence that is God.

I learned from holy women before me that finding God depends on four things: a conscious awareness of the presence of God; the sacralization of life; an attunement to the Holy Spirit; and a sense of place in the universe.

A conscious awareness of the presence of God requires the development of a sincere and serious prayer life that is more reflective, thoughtful and contemplative than it is mere rote and ritual. "Going to church" is not a substitute for putting myself in the presence of God. Turning our minds and hearts over to the God of the universe puts us in the place of that which we seek. The purpose of prayer is not to make God conscious of us; it is to make us conscious of God. It is to attend to the God in whom we live and whose presence we either ignore or expect to find somewhere else.

The sacralization of life requires us, in the words of Benedict of Nursia's fifteen-century-old Rule, to "treat all things as vessels of the altar"—to hold every isolated thing in high regard whatever its use, to treat it gently, to take care of it well whatever its age. It leads us to become part of the holiness of the universe by recognizing each and every element of it as a spark of the Divine. It nurtures in us that sense of the sacred in all things so that the presence of God becomes a fact of life, not a myth to be fabricated. It leads us to save and care for and preserve and respect the goods of material creation so that we can come to respect the spiritual energy that underlies each of them. It is learning to live in sacred space again so that we can be surprised by God. We are part of a holy universe, not its creators and not its rulers. God has done the creating, God does the judging and God waits for us to realize that.

An attunement to the Holy Spirit enables us to hear the word of God in those around us and in the circumstances of our lives—in our culture, in our sexuality, and in the racial makeup that is the raw material of our being. It lies in bringing each of those things to fulfillment—whatever the obstacles to each. Everything we are, everything that is said to us, everything that happens to us is some kind of call from God. In fact, everything that happens is God's call to us either to accept what we should not change or to change what we should not accept so that the Presence of God can flourish where we are. Until we learn to listen to these manifestations of divine presence all around us in life, we need not expect visions.

A sense of our place in the universe is what Chapter Seven of the Rule of Benedict calls "The Twelve Degrees of Humility." In one of the earliest pieces of Western spiritual literature, Benedict is very clear that the beginning of a spiritual life depends on the realization that we live in the womb of God, that we need to admit our struggles, that we need to accept the inconsequential circumstances of life with equanimity, and that we need to cultivate the kind of internal peace that leads us to live gently with the rest of creation, to tread lightly through the universe and to deal tenderly with both ourselves and others.

Finding God is a matter of seeing God where God is, of seeing the God who is in us to sustain us, around us to touch us, before us to beckon us onward in life. Finding God is a matter not of learning to become something we are not but of learning to see what we already know, to touch what we already contain, to recognize what we already have. Finding God is a matter of living every minute of life to its ultimate. "Oh, wonder of wonders," the Zen teacher teaches. "I chop wood. I draw water from the well." Finding God has little to do with church and more to do with becoming the best of everything we are every moment we breathe.

God is not a mystery to be sought in strange places and arcane ways. God is a mystery to be discovered within us and around us. And savored.

12.

What Does It Mean to Be Human?

To ask what it means to be human strikes at the fabric of the soul. The temptation, of course, is to gloss, to idealize. The task, however, requires much more than that. The task is not to rhapsodize; it is to distinguish between the human and the nonhuman, the subhuman that rages under it, taxing our humanity at every turn. Then, the task becomes plain. In Thomas Hardy's words, "If way to the better there be, we must look first at the worst."

The problem with trying to define what it means to be human is that we now take so much of the inhuman for granted. We confuse the meaning of the words "natural" and "human," make synonyms of them. We act as if one is the other. We allow one to be the other. We rip to shreds the ideas each of them masks, forgetting one and surrendering to the other. We call the "natural" human and in one flash of the pen presume we have made it so. We wander in a philosophical maze and never even realize that we are lost.

War is "natural," they tell us. Violence is "natural," they argue. Self-aggrandizement is "natural," they maintain. What they do not say is that just because something is "natural" does not make it human. And then the slippage starts, the desecration of life.

Greed is "only human," they maintain. Sexism is the will of God, they insist. Rape becomes a weapon of war, of "defense," of the humiliation of one male by another at the expense of women. In a mindset such as that, ambition is not only condoned; it is encouraged. Dishonesty becomes the coin of the land. Bankers cheat; brokers steal; presidents lie; and the rest of us lower our standards to meet the norm and concentrate more on survival than we do on life. We begin to pay more attention to what we are getting out of life than what we are putting into it.

We cluck at rape, of course, and shake our heads about genocide and talk about being bored with TV murder trials; we cease to look at the pictures of small, long-lost children, memorialized on milk cartons. We buy more locks and more guns and insurance policies, hire more lawyers. But we change nothing in ourselves, or in anything else. We simply become more and more inured to the "natural," and less and less confident that humanity is a star to be followed or anything more than a brass ring on a boardwalk carousel where fantasy reigns and the process of going someplace is to trace an interminable circle. Humanity goes in and out of focus, blurred always by the "natural" and unconscious of the spiritual that magnetizes it.

But I have seen humanity. I know its face even when I cannot define it. It is blazoned in my mind. It measures my character and condemns my disregard. Anything less than these images disappoint me to this core.

I have a picture in my mind of nuns putting flowers in the gun barrels of Filipino soldiers in Manila who then refused to shoot into the crowd. I still hold in my heart the sight of a young man in Tiananmen Square standing in front of a moving tank that then turned back. I carry the image of men carrying a lone survivor out of a tangle of earthquake wreckage on a swaying overpass that then collapsed. Every time these images flash before my mind I remember that to be human is to give yourself for things far greater than yourself.

I have a memory, too, as a twelve-year-old of crying silently but bitterly, face down into a pillow on the living room floor. That day, my bird, my only life companion, had disappeared up an open flue in our apartment wall. There were visiting relatives in the house, in my bedroom, whom I knew were not to be disturbed. The needs of the guest came first, I had been taught. But when the house was safely dark, I let the pain pour out, not simply for the loss of my dearest possession but also in sorrow for my own carelessness in his regard. Then, suddenly, I felt the covers around me tighten. My mother had gotten in on one side of the mattress, my father on the other, and together they held me all the long and empty night. I learned then that being human meant to enter into someone else's pain.

I heard a young US soldier talk enthusiastically about gunning down Iraqi soldiers from planes as "a turkey shoot." The look of glee in his eyes, the excitement in his voice, while he described spraying frightened men with high-caliber bullets from thousands of feet above them numbed me to the center of my soul. If truth were known, it confused me, too. After all, it was a good thing, wasn't it, that we had "won" a war with so little bloodshed.

Then I read a tale from the Sufi and came to understand where the numbness had come from. Once upon a time there was an old woman who used to meditate early on the bank of the Ganges. One morning, finishing her meditation, she saw a scorpion floating helplessly in the strong current. As the scorpion was pulled closer, it got caught in roots that branched out far into the river. The scorpion struggled frantically to free itself but got more and more entangled.

She immediately stretched herself onto the extended roots and reached out to rescue the drowning scorpion, which as soon as she touched it, stung her. The old woman withdrew her hand, but having regained her balance, once again tried to save the creature. Every time she tried, however, the scorpion's tail stung her so badly that her hands became bloody and her face distorted with pain.

A passerby who saw the old woman struggling with the scorpion shouted, "What's wrong with you, fool? Do you want to kill yourself to save that ugly thing?"

Looking into the stranger's eyes, she answered, "Because it is the nature of the scorpion to sting, why should I deny my own nature to save it?" Then I understood the numbness. Then I learned that Reverence for Life is of the essence of humanity.

And that is what we have lost. We "defend" ourselves by threatening the globe and our own level of civilized humanness with it. We have chosen technological progress and financial profits over the needs of human beings. We have bartered the quality of our own souls; we live the denial of Reverence for Life.

But we have become a society of machines and business degrees, of stocks and bonds, of world power and world devastation, of what works and what makes money. We train our young to get ahead, our middle-aged to consume and our elderly to be silent. We are sophisticated now. We live in stadiums, not galleries. We listen to rap music, not Mozart. We talk about our ideas for getting ahead rather than about our ideas for touching God. We are miles from our roots and light-years away from our upbringings. We have abandoned the concerns of the civilizations before us. We have forsaken the good, the true and the beautiful for the effective, the powerful and the opulent. We have abandoned enoughness for the sake of consumption. We are modern. We are progressive. And we are lost.

So what do I believe in? What do I define as human? I believe in the pursuit of the spiritual, in the presence to pain, and the sacredness of life. Without these, life is useless and humanity a farce.

To be human it is necessary, perhaps, to think again about what matters in life, to ask always why what is, is. To be human is to listen to the rest of the world with a tender heart, and learn to live life with our arms open and our souls seared with a sense of responsibility for everything that is.

Without a doubt, given those criteria, we may indeed not live the "better life," but we may, at the end, at least have lived a fully human one.

13.

Thirst for Beauty, Thirst for Soul

The ancients are clear: No one is sure what beauty really is. "The beauty that addresses itself to the eyes is only the spell of the moment; the eye of the body is not always that of the soul," George Sand wrote in 1872, and the idea seems to be a universal one. However hard we try to make plain to the mind what is plain only to the soul, precision in this area consistently eludes us. But of one thing about beauty, it seems, the world is reasonably certain: We know it when we see it. There is, in Christopher Morley's words, "a secret nerve that answers to the vibrations of beauty." It quivers in the human soul, this nerve. It leads us like a magnet to the pole. It nourishes a flickering life in us and resuscitates whatever it is in the soul that may be dying for lack of reason to exist.

Beauty, unlike anything else in creation, has a reason for existence that goes far beyond function. Beauty is a beacon on the mountain of the mind that brings us home to our best selves. Beauty is that moment of insight in which the genie of a thing is caught in a single flash, a heartbeat of awareness, and made present for eternity. Beauty calls us beyond both the present and the past to that everlasting "Now" where what is can never be dismissed again from the audit of the human enterprise.

Beauty, in other words, lifts life out of the anesthetizing effects of the pedestrian and gives us a reason for going on, for being, for ranging beyond our boundaries, for endeavoring always to be more than we are. It enables us to pause in time long enough to remember that some things are worth striving for, that some things are worth doing over and over again until they become their breathless selves, that some things are beyond our grasp yet within our reach. Beauty brings with it the realization in the midst of struggle, in the depths of darkness, in the throes of ugliness, that the best in life is, whatever the cost, really possible.

It is the artist's task, then, to take us beyond the invisible to the height of consciousness, past the humdrum to the mystical, away from the expedient to the endlessly true. The artist shows us what we thought we could never, perhaps should never, see: the soul of a tree, the suffering of the helpless, the bowels of a color, the brilliance of a darkness that reveals the unconquerable light, a form without failing. The artist takes a piece of life and turns it inside out for us and, in the doing, turns us inside out over it, as well. We look at something for which we have no words and we ache for the voice that can make beauty tangible. We touch the beautiful and reframe our own vision of the world. We see something which we have looked at many times but never really seen before and find ourselves less alone in the universe because someone else has touched what we have touched, felt what we have felt, known what we have known. Then, we are never the same again because we have seen a rent in the fabric of eternity, gotten an insight into timelessness, come face to face with the ultimate. Then, we have seen a bit of the Beauty out of which beauty comes.

Beauty is a deeply spiritual experience. It shouts to us always, "More. There is yet more." That God created out of nothing we can understand. Real spiritual insight lies in coming to realize that the artist creates out of the Nothingness that is God, the beginning of the beginning, the end of the end. Kahlil Gibran says of it: "Beauty is eternity gazing at itself in a mirror." The artist takes the beauty that is and gives it visibility, makes it present to us in ways that astound, that move, that arrest our free-float through time with a cognizance of the eternal. In the artist is an eye for the things of godliness, stark and unrelenting, clear and unblinking. In the artist, truth is not consumed by prettiness or being by repetition. Those who contrive to capture beauty for the world by chaining it to itself, by consuming it under one form, by entrapping it in a single configuration, by wrenching it to any single, isolated design only manage, in the end, to smother the very thing they set out to unleash. Then beauty turns into conformity and crumbles to dust. Then we do not have art, we do not have beauty, we have, at best, only nicety. We do not have the creative process, we have only cheap reproductions of what was once a soul-riving moment. Instead, somewhere out there beyond the artist—somewhere deep inside the artist—there is a single unsaid thought, an uncultivated statement, a piercing unasked question, a primitive unseen reality, an idea that comes out of the center of God once and only once in this particular form and which, once rendered, takes humanity back to the heart of God again.

Beauty is a moment in time that must be captured so that the human heart can, in the midst of pain and despair, cling to the notion that that which is capable of bearing beauty is capable of bringing new life, is capable of pervading the world, is able by penetrating our own souls to penetrate the ugliness of a world awash in the cheap, the tawdry, the imitative, the excessive and the cruel.

Beauty demands discipline. Where there is too much noise, too much color, too many curlicues, too much posturing, too garish a shape, too intrusive an element, too corrupting a presence, beauty has been prostituted for spectacle. "Nothing in excess," the ancients called it. Everything "just right," we call it. But there is so little that is "just right" in a world suckled on

violence and conceived through greed, bereft of beauty and surrendered to pragmatism. Everywhere harmony, proportion, truth
die from discord, from the ways things should never really be,
from the failure to find grandeur in the landscape of humanity,
in the observance of the obvious. The memory of the Holocaust,
the sight of "the geography of evil" in South Africa, the shock
of genocide in Bosnia, the trivialization of women the world
over, the disregard for children everywhere as we pursue power
and profit in a patriarchal system, measure the paucity of our
souls, demand that we ask again the questions "What is it to be
fully human?" and "How do we develop it?" At a moment in
history in which the destruction of the planet and the extinc-
tion of peoples has been raised to high art, to levels beyond the
realm of human imagination only fifty years ago, those may be
the core questions of the twenty-first century. And art may be
their answer.

Who can bring us back from the brink of our own destruction but the artist, the one whose eye is open and whose heart
is true? Who can make us see "rightness" again but the one who
causes us to see rightness in every single cast of the eye? How
can we save the human soul unless we resuscitate the human
imagination grown weary from the technical and jaded by the
false claims of the commercial?

Imagination allows us to rethink everything we ever knew, to
start over one more time, to begin again, to dare to be new, to
encapsulate the old in brave new ways. How can we hone the
ability to see beyond the actual with its tawdry compromise of
vision to the pragmatic of the ideal, the place in the heart where
we know that what must be can be, if we do not release the
imagination of the artist, the one who pursues beauty, perception, depth and discernment as a way of life, as a sacred vocation?
The one who walks into darkness and brings the light of insight
there for the rest of us to see? Indeed, the artist is the eyes of a
blind world.

A great deal passes for imagination today that could never have been possible before the advent of computer models, movie sets and "paint by numbers" kits, however popular such things may be. But there is a knowledge about beauty in the human spirit that no amount of other knowledge can discount. We know without doubt that there are a number of things that attempt to pass for beauty which, whatever the glitz that surrounds them, are mere shadows of the real thing. Fashion comes and goes and is called "beautiful" but the world only yawns at it. Styles take possession of a culture and are proclaimed to be "beautiful" but for the most part we simply mark them historically and move on. Trends consume a genre and become for a time its standard of excellence, the measure of its beauty, but though we may mark their coming with scientific accuracy we are just as sure of their going, as well. Though fashions and styles and trends cater to passing fads and bring attention to what may otherwise be empty and create a class of artifacts that make the run of every chain store hotel, restaurant and bedroom community in the nation, no one calls them art. The fact is that such assembly line memorabilia are at best cheap substitutes for vision. They lack at core that touch of soul, that gleam of eternity, that glimpse of the timelessness of the present that makes art, art. We know without doubt that it is only when we see what we have never seen before—a flash of essence, a flicker of truth—but which, down deep, we have always known ourselves to be seeking that we have really found art, have really discovered beauty.

Clearly, what is copied is not art, it is at most craft. What is not spiritually penetrating is not art, it is at best formula fiction. What is simply more of the same—no uniqueness intended, no gasp of realization arrested in mid-flight—is not art, it is at best a cartoon character of life lived without the inner cleansing that comes with a shocking consciousness of the present moment.

Art is, indeed, the sacrament of awareness, a trumpet call to every soul to come to life again and see, to rise to the heights

of itself again and become, to strive for more than the lowest
level of existence and to transcend the banal. It is not negative
asceticism, not the destruction of life, that saves the world, it is
the raising of the mind to humanity's highest aspirations.

Art takes us into the center of ourselves, to both the sanctuary and the cesspool of humanity, and binds us in that way to
the whole human race. Beauty is, invariably, the best of what
we hope for everywhere. It carries with it always the character
of the ultimate: the ultimate in humanity, the ultimate in being,
the ultimate in whatever it is in which we have seen a glimpse
of ultimate goodness.

Beauty takes many forms. I have seen many of them, disarm-
ingly simple and boldly compelling, both where I expected
them and where I did not: I saw a Mexican Indian woman, nine
members of her family assassinated in the mountains of Chiapas,
stand at their grave site, infant in arms, hard-jawed but soft of
eye and still open to life. That was beautiful.

I watched, too, as lines and lines of working-class Italians stood
waiting for the lights to go on that would illuminate for too
precious a moment Michelangelo's "Moses" in the small, dark
chapel of St. Peter in Chains in Rome. The awe in their eyes was
as beautiful as the sinews in the marbled arms, the big-boned
kneecaps of the Moses above them. Both were full of feeling,
both held promise of the kind of energy that can come only
from the depths of the human heart.

Once I stood, hands clasped behind me, and stared at eye
level into Rembrandt's "Journey into Egypt," black on black on
black, one small light glowing in the darkness of the exile. That
was beauty beyond beauty, the vision of someone who had seen
more in the wilderness of flight than I had ever known was there.

And I have with my own hands turned a turntable that held
a vase, one of its kind, in the dust-filled, cluttered, cement-
block studio where Brother Thomas, our monastery's artist-in-
residence, throws and shapes and glazes and fires his pottery. Its

colors shuddered into one another. Its weight hung suspended on a sliver of a base, poised in mid-air, light and heavy at the same time, stable and airy at once, strikingly true, totally isolate, in a sea of sensuousness that spoke only of the spiritual. It was vastness I was seeing, nude and total, universal and particular all at once. It was tradition revered and imagination run amok—a classic Chinese form alive again, the ancient made new, dazzlingly young again, a taste of forever, an expectation of the eternal. I stepped back, took my hands off this wild excursion into being, knew in the center of my brain that here touch was sacrilege and that such a sacrilege was beautiful.

There is no end of beauty, never enough of it, always a dearth of it, forever a need for it, in our time more than most when images are cosmic, instant and enduring. We are immersed in ugliness. We are afloat in the bland. We are awash in the trite. We are a people with more commitment to function than to soul. We want things to work rather than to be. Those criteria, those judgments mark our culture, make it characterless, doom it to the mundane, erase it from the roll of those civilizations that mark the real development of humankind.

In our time, we care more for destruction than for development. We target the world for death and call our blasphemy of beauty "defense." We are a universe of broken bodies, a galaxy of fractured minds. Such a society has lost respect for beauty and so has no respect for life. Such a society weeps for lack of art and has no idea for what it grieves. What is needed if this world of ours is to survive the twenty-first century is surely the heart that is true, the seeing heart, the artist's heart.

There are cures, of course, for such deprivation of spirit. We could take down the billboards that turn the landscape into a junkyard of old ideas. We could refuse to allow people to turn marble statues into plastic replicas. We could study the order, the harmony, the proportion of a flower. We could strain our eyes to look for what is beneath the obvious in the wrinkles of age, the meaning in every moment, the ultimate in every possibility, the essence of every encounter. Or, we could simply own one soul-shattering piece of art ourselves, put it up in a solitary site as mute conviction of the mediocre around it, place it over and against the fashionable cliches which normally surround us. We could let it seep into the center of the self until we find that we can never be satisfied again, tranquilized again, by the adultery of intelligence around us, until we ourselves come to realize that only the true is really beautiful.

The problem is a simple one: What we do not nourish within ourselves cannot exist in the world around us because we are its microcosm. We cannot bemoan the loss of quality in our world and not ourselves seed the beautiful in our wake. We cannot decry the loss of the spiritual and continue to function only on the level of the expedient. We cannot hope for fullness of life without nurturing fullness of soul. We must seek beauty, study beauty, surround ourselves with beauty. To revivify the soul of the world, we must become beauty. Where we are must be more beautiful than it was before our coming.

14.

God Become Infinitely Larger

Two seekers inspire a sense of the possibility and potential of this topic, and shape these reflections of mine on "God at 2000."

The first is an old Sufi who was found scratching through the sand in the middle of the road. "What are you doing, Sufi?" pilgrims asked as they passed him, digging and scratching, on their way to the temple.

"I am looking for the treasure I have lost," the old man said. So the pilgrims, good people all, dropped to their knees to help—sifting sand, digging under stones, and sweating under the waxing midday sun. Finally, hungry, soaking wet, and exhausted, one of the travelers said to him at last,

"Sufi, are you sure you lost your treasure here?"

And the old man said, "Oh my! No. I did not lose my treasure here. I lost it over there on the other side of those mountains."

"Well, if you lost it on the other side of the mountains," the people shouted at him, "why, in the name of Allah, are you looking for it here?"

And the old man said, "I am looking for it here because there is more light here."

My second guide through the complexities of this question is the seeker who asked the holy one: "How are we to seek union with God?"

And the holy one said, "The harder you seek, the more distance you create between God and you."

"Then what does one do about the distance?" the disciple persisted.

And the holy one said, "Understand that it isn't there."

"But does that mean that God and I are one?" the seeker asked.

And the holy one said: "Not one. Not two."

"But how is that possible?" the seeker said.

And the holy one said: "The sun and its light, the ocean and the wave, the singer and his song—Not one. Not two."[1]

What I have learned about God after a lifetime of seeking is that first, God must be sought in the light, and that secondly, God does not have to be found.

If there is anything in the world, however, that may deserve our pity, it may well be the very idea of "God." What else in the history of humankind has been more reviled as fraud, more ridiculed as unprovable or, on the other hand, more glorified out of existence—more condemned to unattainable remoteness—than the notion of God?

The wag wrote once: "First God created us, and then we created God." The insight may be far too true to ignore, and the consequences of it far too distancing to celebrate.

The marketplace is, in fact, full of ideas about God—religious tradition itself not the least of the purveyors of them. Some of these ideas have been helpful to the development of a God-life within me, some of them not.

Whatever the images of God we offer, whatever the effects of them spiritually and socially, I have come to the conclusion over the years that it is precisely our idea of God that is the measure of our spiritual maturity. What we believe about God colors

---

[1] Anthony DeMello, *One Minute Wisdom* (Anand, India: Gujarat Sahitya Prakash, 1985), 34.

everything we do in the name of God, everything we think about other people, everything we determine about life itself.

And it is not—this consciousness of God—exceptional. No, in the long light of human history, it is not belief in God that sets us apart. Belief in the existence of God may be the very least term of the equation. It is certainly not unique to us, to the West, to Christianity, or even to this sophisticated time in history, the character of which we like to consider so advanced, so "enlightened." In fact, all peoples on earth have come to the juncture where only God is an answer to questions for which there is no answer. All peoples on earth have found their way to God, to some kind of God, to some answer to the universe that is above and outside themselves.

It is not the idea of God that sets us apart in the history of humanity. It is the kind of God in which we choose to believe that in the end makes all the difference. And each of us fashions a private God the face of whom shapes our own.

Some believe, for instance, in a God of wrath and so themselves become wrathful with others as a result. Some believe in a God who is indifferent to the world and, when they find themselves alone—as all of us do at some time or another—they shrivel up and die inside from the indifference they feel in the world around them.

Some believe in a God who makes traffic lights turn green and so become the children of magical coincidence in a world crying out for clear-eyed, hard-headed, responsible shapers of this clay called life.

Some believe in a God of laws, and crumble in spirit and psyche when they themselves break those laws or else become even more stern in demanding from others standards they themselves cannot keep. They conceive of God as the manipulator of the universe rather than its ground. God, they hold, is the part of the scene that lies behind the objects in the forefront. They project onto God humanity's own small desires and indignities and needs.

I have known all of those Gods in my own life and they have all failed me.

I have learned that law-keeping did not satisfy my need for meaning. I learned that, to be properly wicked, it was not necessary to break the law—just to keep it to the letter! I have learned that the fear of wrath did not seduce me to love. I have learned that God the distant doer of unpredictable and arbitrary magic failed to engage or enliven my soul. I have learned that life was surely about far more important things than that. If the question, then, is "Who is God for me in the year 2000?" my answer has to be: "God is not the God I thought I knew in 1950."

One of the best things I was ever taught about God was by a philosophy professor who told us that we could not "think" God. And he was obviously right, though clearly, think God we did— and aplenty. In my own case, God has been a changing, moving, inviting, disturbing and totally engrossing mystery, and the more I thought about God, it seemed, the less I knew God at all.

I have feared the God of judgment and been judgmental of others. I have used God to get me through life. I have called the intolerable "God's will" and called our failure to stop evil God's failure to stop evil. I have expected God to be the crutch that would make the unbearable bearable, and, as a result, I often failed to take steps to change life either for myself or others when injustice masked itself as God's will and oppression as God's judgment.

I thought about God "out there" and became blind to the God within me. And so, thinking of God as far away, I failed to make God present to others who were in my presence.

I have, in other words, allowed God to be mediated to me through images of God foreign to the very idea of God:

- God the puppeteer, who created free will but takes it back when it gets inconvenient;

- God the potentate, whose interest is self-love;
- God the persecutor, who created life to trap it in its own ignorance;
- God the mighty male to whom obedience, subservience and deference were the only proper response, and in whose being women were apparent only for their absence.

I have come to the conclusion, after a lifetime of looking for God, that a divinity such as these is simply a graven image of ourselves, not a God big enough to believe in.

All of those images, ironically, actually blocked the image of the presence of God in life for me.

All of them made a mockery of the very definition of God—the fullness of being—the one who, having created us, wills us well and not woe, good and not grief, and all of us fullness of life, not some of us inert and invisible nothingness.

Indeed, it is the God in whom we choose to believe that determines the rest of life for us. In our conception of the nature of God lies the kernel of the spiritual life. Surely, no one really believes that this conference is about God at 2000. This conference is about us at 2000!

Made in the image of God, we grow in the image of the God we make for ourselves. They told us that God was creator and judge. They drew pictures to prove the point. But they forgot to tell us what they could not draw. They neglected to tell us what the philosophy professor knew: that God is what we cannot think and what we cannot not think at the same time.

We have, obviously, in our attempt to understand God as personal, configured the Godhead to be a person writ larger than ourselves. We have seen in that limited conception both the best and the worst, both the most limitless and the most partial of ourselves. To make this partiality an absolute warps both God and us. I substitute my own limitations for the limitlessness of God.

I learned as life went by that the God I make will be the God I seek, the spiritual life I live, and the quality of my own heart. Until I discover the God in whom I myself believe, then, until I unmask the God who lives in my own heart, regardless of the panoply of other God-images around me, I will never understand another thing about my own life. Or, as Woody Allen said, "Confidence is what we have until we understand the problem."

I knew, when I looked back, that it was when my God was harsh judge that I lived in a guilt so unquenchable that it blocked the fullness of whatever goodness might be in me and most of the hope in me, as well. I knew I could not possibly measure up to the smallness of the God I'd made.

I myself have lived in those boxes of sins where the rules I kept and the rituals I practiced were my gods. They were more important to me than the people I met who, helpless, could do nothing but wait for God to work through me, through my devotion to God on their behalf. Unlike the God of the prodigal son, this small God of mine shut doors in the face of the ones not as plumb, not as rigid as I, so that in my rigidity I skewed the very spiritual course I was intent to follow.

The checklists and the dos and don'ts had become my God, until those gods waxed and waned and disappeared into the dust out of which they had been formed.

In the period of my life when my God became Holy Nothingness—not so much imaginary as simply a philosophical question of no great immediate interest and even less conviction—I lived a life of cosmic loneliness. The great questions of life became What's it all about? And why bother? And who cares anyway?

I discovered the chasm of the soul that comes when God is too high to care and too far away to notice; when God the vending machine did not answer in the way I wanted; when God the judge let evil go by unchallenged; when my God was taunter and bully, who tweaked and teased me with temptations rather than give me the experiences I needed to bring me to what Julian of Norwich had experienced, the very heights of mystical consciousness. I was struggling through life impaled on the pin of a grinning giant called God!

I learned as life went on that clearly the professor was correct: I could not think God. But, I have now learned, the professor was also incorrect at the same time. Not to be able to think about God is only to make God unthinkable; it is not to make God unreal. The great spiritual truth, I learned over the years, is that, indeed, we cannot think God. We can only know God. And when we do think God into some single separate stultifying shape, it is only a sign that we now run the risk of knowing God less and less.

Each of these separate dimensions of God—justice and law and reason and omnipotence and a kind "tsk-tsking" love at a distance—marks a stage of my own life: Each of them has been a highway marker through a complex of religious practices. Each of them good for the sake of the focus they gave me but false when they became an end in themselves and dimmed the sacramental nature—the divine depths—of the rest of life.

I searched for God and found the God who was a tribal God, the God who was a Catholic God, the God who was on our side not theirs, the God who was white and American and male—definitely male—the God they called key, door, wind, spirit, dove and rock, but never, never, mother! But over the years, faced with one question after another—What was it to be a woman? What was it to step into outer space? What was it to see goodness where once I had been told only faithlessness abounded?—I became more and more convinced that God was to be found in other places and that it was only the search itself that could possibly save me from the worst consequences of each.

I have seen God grow. Or maybe I have seen me grow and couldn't tell the difference.

I have abandoned God the stern father who had no time for human nonsense and little time for women either. I have abandoned God the cloud-sitter who keeps count of our childish stumbles toward spiritual adulthood in order to exact fierce retribution from humans for being human. And I have seen all those fragments of the face of God dissolve into the mist of impossibility.

I am more and more convinced that those Gods do not exist, never did exist, must not exist if God is really God.

But when such small ideas die, with what great thoughts shall we replace them?

I have become sure that if all I know about God is that my God is the fullness of life and the consummation of hope, the light on the way, and the light at the end, I will live my life in the consciousness of God and goodness everywhere, obscure at times, perhaps, but never wholly lacking.

So now God, that old rascal, is doing it again. I am moving in my heart from God as a trophy to be won, or a master, however benign, to be pacified, to God as cosmic unity and everlasting light.

The change has been gradual but very, very clear. It has come at the juncture of five divides, all seemingly separate, but all of a piece: spiritual tradition, personal experience, science, globalism and feminism. These have all come together in my life to show me a God whom I cannot think but do deeply know to be true. I have learned from them all to know a greater God than I had been given. Let me explain.

The spiritual tradition that guides me is an ancient one: In the Rule of Benedict of Nursia (a Catholic document written in the sixth century and still the way of life for thousands of monastics today) chapter seven—"On Humility"—sums up Benedict's spiritual theology. In light of the spirituality of the last several hundred years, it is at least startling if not unsettling.

The first degree of humility, the first step on the way to God, is to have always before our eyes what the ancients call the fear of God—what we know as the sense of God, the awe of God, the awareness of God, the presence of God.

The religious culture of Benedict's time was immersed in merit theology, a theology that sought deliverance from damnation by earning God. So many masses equal so much union with God, so many Rosaries equals so many units of God, so many penances and sacrifices and formulas of the faith equals so much fullness of God. Into this religious culture came an astounding revelation.

The first step to union with God is knowing that you already have God, you already enjoy God, you already contain within yourself the life that is God.

Both the Jewish mystic Isaac Luria (1534–1572) and the Catholic theologian Pierre Teilhard de Chardin (1881–1955) speak of the sparks of God—the residue of the creator in all of us—as common to the entire human race. The idea goes back to Moses at a flaming bush; to Jesus aglow on a mountaintop; to Benedict's first degree of humility that teaches us the grandeur of us all; to the mystic Julian of Norwich, who saw God as nurturing mother and "all that is" in an acorn. It links us in turn to the here and now, to a kind of spirituality that breaks down barriers and jumps boundaries. This is a spirituality in which I know that wherever I am, whatever state of mind, God is the spirit with me and the life in me. God is there for the taking, God is the air I breathe and God is the path I take. God is the womb in which I live. As the Zen proverb reads: "If enlightenment is not where you are standing, where will you look?" This was Benedictine spirituality, steeped in the Jewish and Christian scriptures, that changed my awareness of the living God as alive around me, existing beyond me and breathing within me.

There were other things as well. Personal experience, science, globalism and feminism that came to crumble, wash away and replace a God made small by puny ideas cast in puny images.

My ideas about God shook themselves free of legal lists and the golden calves of denominationalism, maleness and race, but it took another half a lifetime to come to trust them.

As a young teenager, kneeling in a dark cathedral one night, with no illumination in the church but the sanctuary lamp, I had an experience of intense light. I was thirteen years old and totally convinced that, whatever it was and wherever it came from, the light was God. Perhaps it was a good janitor working late, or a bad switch that did not work at all, a startling insight given to a young woman, given gratuitously. I did not know then and I don't know now. But I did know that the light was God and that God was light.

I was never able to forget that experience, nor did I ever talk about it, until this very moment. And I only do it now because I'm here in private conversation with a few thousand of my most intimate friends, and then only because I was confronted by the honest question, "Who is God for you?" I have few classical answers, but it demands an honest response.

After that experience, whenever God was shrunk to meet someone's then current need to control or frighten or cajole me, whenever God the vending machine or God the theological Santa Claus did not give me what I wanted, or whenever God the judge let evil go by unchallenged, I knew now that God was bigger than these gods, because I was never able to stop feeling the unshaped, uncontrolled, undiminished light.

For me as an adult, two different texts confirmed the image of God that I learned that night in the cathedral and lived for years in the presence of God in a Benedictine community. The first text that called me to images beyond images was the Hebrew–Christian scriptures, an ancient commentary and testimony on God's ways in the world. The scriptures showed me the God who would not test Job; who debated with Abraham about the degree of sinlessness it would take to save the city, and lost; the God whose own identity was revealed to Moses simply, profoundly, as "I Am Who I Am," "I Will Be What I Will Be," and to Jonah as "mercy upon mercy upon mercy," and in the Jesus of the Mount of Transfiguration bathed in light. This was a God without a face of any color or gender, a God who came in fire and light, God with us—Emmanuel—but unseen, God with me, but hidden in the obvious. That God, I knew, lived in the light. And the light, I could feel, was inside of me.

The second text was a tiny little book by Jean Pierre de Caussade called *Abandonment to Divine Providence*. It brought me beyond the God of the distant and the partial, the punitive and the parental. It kept an ancient stream of thought alive under the avalanche of legalism, denominationalism and doctrinal rules. The title of the book sounds like some kind of professional quietism or personal masochism but it brought the distant God as close to me as the minute I am in. Then all the thinking stopped and the knowing began, and the light burned the images away.

After that growing awareness of the immersing presence of God, I became conscious of two other present and obvious but long-standing threats to traditional religious belief. Each became a spiritual revelation to me that was both logical and undeniable.

The first burst of insight was science, once the champion of the "material" and the skeptic of the spiritual. Science had made the split between the two seem irreconcilable. But then scientists unexpectedly discovered that the only difference between solids and space was the degree to which the same atoms that composed both were packed more or less closely together. The old line—the heretofore uncompromising line, the dividing line, between matter and spirit—had suddenly blurred. How could we really separate the two? So why not the material in the spiritual and the spiritual in the material? I, too, learned that the God who could not be verified was no greater an assumption than the scientific "facts" of modern physics, astronomy or cosmology. These could not be verified experientially either, unless you know someone who has walked to Mars with a pedometer in her hand.

The mathematical findings of quantum physics, chaos theory and the Big Bang forced classic scientific theory to turn in a different direction. The limits of knowledge ran out. Knowledge of the unlimited consumed us, and broke open our spirits to spiritual things greater than ourselves. A universe which, in 1900, we had taught with confidence had one galaxy, the Milky Way, now revealed to the telescope's eye in the year 2000 that there were at least forty billion galaxies out there. In such a world newly revealed as this, even the agnostic physicist Stephen Hawking asked in wonder what it was that "breathes fire into the equations?"[2] Who or what is the beginning behind the universe? The energy in the eternal expansion?

Suddenly science was a great spiritual teacher for me. Science became the guide to a God far greater than the God of petty sins and trivial traps and privatized religion. God was the God of the universe whose creating life lives in us, in me and in others, and in the stars, and whose light is bringing us home.

The second burst of insight across the sensors of my soul that changed the image of God for me was far less ethereal than science and cosmology. The melting of national boundaries and the free flow of peoples and ideas across the globe introduced for me a new kind of cognitive dissonance. The white, male, Catholic, American God was suddenly suspect: Were all these others—over four-fifths of the world—really "Godless," without revelation, without any or all truth? Globalism, I came to realize, was a less startling, a less dramatic revelation of the presence of

---

[2] Stephen Hawking, *A Brief History of Time* (London: Bantam Press, 1988), 174.

God. Perhaps in the end it was, at least for me, an even more revealing one than scientific equations could ever be.

Sprung from the Catholic ghetto, however good that may have been in my spiritual formation, I found God at work everywhere, revealed everywhere, known everywhere. The old joke about God warning every new person at the gates of Paradise to tiptoe past Room 10 on the way to their heavenly quarters because the Catholics in Room 10 thought they were the only people there took on new meaning. So did Jesus' insight that in the house of God there were many dwelling places (John 14:2), Benedict's vision of having seen "the whole world in a single ray of light," and the injunction of Vatican Council II to "accept whatever was true in other religions." Clearly then, something was happening to me. I had learned the greatest truth of all: God was bigger than parochialism. God had many faces. God had many names. God was a magnet in many hearts, all of which, according to the Parliament of the World's Religions meeting in Cape Town in December 1999, embraced a common global ethic: not to lie, not to steal, not to kill, and not to exploit others sexually. Or to put it in more religious terms: to hold all life as sacred, to honor every truth, to deal with all people justly and to love all life rightly. Clearly, the God of differences spoke in one voice, under whatever form that God might be enshrined, anywhere, everywhere.

So, as my world became smaller, God became infinitely larger. God became present for me not just everywhere, but in everyone, in many ways. God became a cataract of otherness, the likes of which I had never dreamed. God, as Anselm said in the eleventh century, had become for me "that than which nothing greater can be thought."

The third burst of insight was ecofeminism, the growing awareness that both an androcentric (male centered) and an anthropocentric (human centered) world are insufficient, even warped, explanations of life if God is really the fullness of being and no single being is the fullness of God.

When the question is "Are women fully human?" and the scientific answer is a resounding yes; when the scriptural explanation of creation is Adam's declaration that Eve is "bone of my bone, flesh of my flesh," someone just like me; when human beings as the top of the food chain will be the first to go if the planet is degraded; when nothing on earth is dependent on human life for its existence but humans are dependent for theirs on everything else on the planet; and if God, to be God, must be pure spirit, then Augustine's hierarchy of being—maleness and a God made in a male image—has got to be at best suspect, at least incomplete, and in the end bogus.

This male construct of a male God in a male-centered world is no picture of God at all. God is not maleness magnified. God is life without end: all life, in everything, in everyone, in men and women, and in women and men. The light of the divine shines everywhere and has no gender, no single pronoun, no one image.

Life for me has been one long struggle between those limited and myopic images of God and the lifelong prevailing sense of a far greater experience, a more encompassing presence, called God.

If the question is "Who is God for you in the year 2000?" then for me at least—in the face of new glimpses into the universe, the findings of science, the continuing insights of an ancient tradition, the piercing experience of light, the many faces of God around the globe and the revelations of ecofeminism—the answer is certainly, "God is not now who God was for me in 1950." The God at the other swing of my trapeze is fierce but formless presence, undying light in darkness, eternal limitlessness, common consciousness in all creation, an inclusiveness greater than doctrines or denominations, who calls me beyond and out of my limits.

The only proper response to that, as far as I'm concerned, is, "Thank God. Thank God. Thank God."

I have learned clearly that in this new world I must allow no one to draw too small a God for me.

We must know that we have already found what we seek. "Not one. Not two."

And we must realize that, for the sake of the people, for the sake of the planet, for the sake of the empowering presence of God in an increasingly godless world, we must search for God with all the new lights we have.

As Augustine concluded at the end of his own struggle between the intellectual and the religious images of God, "It is better to find you, God, and leave the questions unanswered, than to find answers without finding you."

15.

Dear Sisters and Brothers
of South America

I am writing to you as a citizen of the empire who like you is trying to survive in a world not of our making, not of our heart. I, and many like me in the United States, now find themselves— in our own country—aliens in a foreign land.

I am one American among many whose heart transcends the national boundaries of the United States, and whose soul sees God at work everywhere, in everyone, in languages and liturgies not my own.

I am one of those whose mind reels at the sight of a globe made obscenely rich for some and sinfully poor for others. I shrink at the thought of whole segments of the globe being gobbled up by the greed of international corporations aided and abetted by the power of the governments behind them. I join small group after small group who spend themselves to stop the US juggernaut and live with the frustrations of our failure.

I suffer for those in my own country whose very livelihoods are being ruthlessly outsourced so that US corporations can make obscene profits in obscene ways; can pilfer profits from the pockets of people who have worked hard all their lives only to be abandoned in the end by their own people.

Most of all, I weep for the fact that so many good people here in the land of well-meaning but sleeping giants see none of that.

The people of the United States are good, hardworking and generous people, who since WWII have been taught to define themselves in messianic proportions. What we have not been taught is to be self-critical. Having bested raging disregard for humanity in Germany, having blocked the absorption of Europe into a Germanic Empire, the intended assimilation of Asia into a Japanese one and the hope of collapsing Africa into an Italian one, we came to consider our own virtue as frozen in time. We failed to realize that the power we wrested from the powers of evil in Europe could in the end intoxicate our own sense of self, confuse our own goodness and blind us as a people to the evil latent in our own success.

When a people is imbued with the notion that they are unassailably great and good, self-criticism is out of the question. As a result, the distance between our assumptions about the nature of our system and the reality of our lives can be light-years away from reality.

In the United States, Americans live on certain unquestionable absolutes. They believe with the naivete of children that Americans have never—would never—hurt anyone—despite our own history of segregation and Western territorial expansion that destroyed the Indian culture, wrested its lands and demoralized its peoples.

They are firm in their certainty that Americans have made the world better for everyone—despite our history of economic exploitation of global resources, and our "outsourcing" of menial jobs to women and small children around the world at slave wages.

They are sure that the American press is the only free press in the world—despite the fact that it took years for us to be told as a people that the government lied to us to get us into Vietnam, that, at very best, the dropping of the second atomic bomb at

Nagasaki was purely experimental, and that, as anyone with common sense would know, given the failure of UN inspectors to find anything of major military threat in Iraq, intelligence that is ten years old is not "intelligence" at all. It is at best an excuse to do what you have already decided to do, with or without the intelligence it would take to even begin to justify such an invasion of a sovereign nation.

And now we are even being told that the reason people are resisting our incursion into Iraq is because "they"—whoever "they" happen to be that day—are "evil," "barbarians," and "haters of freedom."

It is a sad and sorry state to be in when you are a citizen of what has been thought to be one of the truest democracies in the world.

We have been suckled on answers that have nothing to do with the real questions because all too many of the real questions exist outside this country. Questions are not our charisma because we are still running on old answers.

The real question is, Why are masses of people who work for the very corporations that once made US citizens rich, poor to the point of destitution? The old answer we have given ourselves for generations is that, unlike us and our immigrant ancestors and us, they do not work as hard as we do.

We fail to realize that even in this country the kinds of jobs that made our largely illiterate and uneducated forebears financially stable—mining, small farms, street sweeping, track laying and large-scale assembly lines—do not exist in this new generation. The tracks are laid, the mines are closed, the farms have been swallowed up in agri-business, machines, not people, sweep the streets and do the dishes now. Even assembly lines have given way to mechanized manufacturing. A technological world finds itself on the brink of creating a permanent underclass and the answer we give poor people is to tear down the welfare system and tell them that they must find jobs in economies that don't have any for them.

The question is, Why is half the world starving when as a nation we have the money and the means to banish hunger from the face of the earth? The answer we argue is that the United States gives more money in foreign aid than any other nation on earth.

Yet, of the twenty-two major donor nations of the world, the United States ranks twenty-two out of twenty-two in per capita foreign aid—and most of that military, not agricultural—though citizens of the United States staunchly, stubbornly, believe that we lead the list! The point is that we have not begun to give what people really need now.

The question is, Why are indigenous lands being devoured by corporations everywhere and poor people left to drift across the globe with the seasons, sleeping in fields, looking for latrines, bent over in the hot sun picking produce that whites will not pick? And in a nation that without these workers would itself lack basic civic services, why is it that government provides them no medical insurance, no legal protections from abuse, no civil rights? Isn't this modern slavery? Isn't this economic colonialism? And if so, why don't the freest people in the world see it? The answer we give ourselves is that those people have never bothered to develop their resources.

We forget that this country alone owns, hoards or consumes two-thirds of the resources of the world, resources that otherwise would be used for the development of other nations besides our own.

The real question is, What responsibilities do the elites of the world have to the people of the world upon whom their riches depend? The old answer is far too commonly an appeal to rugged individualism—if other people really wanted to get rich, they could—or to a tired echo of the Protestant work ethic—

God blesses the good—or to an arrogant reliance on distorted stereotypes of the ignorant foreigner.

"We have managed," I pointed out in a public lecture one day, "to export our industries but we haven't figured out yet, it seems, how to export our salary levels, our pension plans, our paid vacations or our medical insurance." A businessman in the back of the hall was outraged at the very thought of my criticizing US business practices around the world. "Well, they are certainly better off with our jobs than without them, aren't they?" he argued back. "Let me get this straight," I said. "Aren't you saying that they are better off with our injustice than without it?" And his answer to me was that we can't do more because "higher wages wouldn't be right for 'those' people in 'that' culture." As if housing and clothes and shoes for a baby can possibly be improper to anybody's culture.

The question is, How is that a country that claims to operate under the rule of law refuses with impunity to honor international law, makes the abuse of prisoners a military tactic, teaches torture to other nations at its vaunted School of the Americas—renamed "The Western Hemisphere Institute of Security Operations"—and then defies the international community by refusing to recognize the right of an International Military Tribunal to prosecute Americans, too, for war crimes?

And the answer is that we are rich enough, big enough and powerful enough to ignore international law. The answer is that we call other people "evil." We label the unarmed resistance of poor nations "terrorism" because it targets civilians. Then, at the same time, we fund state terrorism—with all its "shock and awe"—that both kills civilians and damages the infrastructure, government and culture of a people for generations to come.

We must stop stirring up a hatred of poor people's guerrilla fighters and start asking ourselves why it is that children danced in the streets of Pakistan when the Twin Towers fell in New York

City. We must build a world based on equity, not on our new foreign legions.

We must together build a world so just that frustration is no excuse for terrorism. We must begin to admit that though there is no justification for terrorism, there is too often a serious explanation for it. Just war is only for nations of equal might. Terrorism is what you get when the strong wreak crass and continual injustice on the weak.

Most of all, we must remember that of the twenty-four nations bombed by the United States after 1946, not one of them developed and maintained a democratic system as a result of it. We are a globe full of differences, a holy Tower of Babel meant by God to be conscience and companion, support and sign of truth to one another. Only mutual respect of those differences will ever bring peace, justice and world community. If there were such a thing as a just war with today's globe-destroying armaments, it would be only for nations of equal might.

So what is the answer to this rise of the new imperialism and the threat of the new empire? You are. I am. Governments everywhere are in collusion or in fear. The rich in mine are manipulating, buying off, pressuring the rich in yours. It is, then, you and I who must stand together.

This is an empire that is not without heart. It is an empire without insight. The people themselves will listen if you and I will only cry out to them.

This is not an empire without conscience. It is an empire without real global information. The people need to know what is being done in our name and they must hear it from us every day, in every way possible. We must not be afraid to speak out. We must only be afraid of becoming what we hate.

This is not an empire without soul. It is an empire without the hint of an idea that its ideals—personal freedom, economic independence, religious toleration—may be holy but the present implementation of the ideas that drive them are narcissistic. The people of the United States must be brought to see that what is good for us is not necessarily good for the rest of the world. What we want—strawberries in wintertime and cheap shoes all the time—is not necessarily ours to have unless we are willing to pay to others who supply those things what we are willing to pay ourselves. What we desire we do not have the right to get—without counting the cost to others.

We must bind together, you and I, to stand up, to speak out, to say our truth, to cite our experience, to demand our due. We must say no to this emperor, yes, but most of all, we must make our appeal to the people of the United States whose own lives are at risk because of a government whose god is oil, whose shrine is money, and whose creed is the civil religion of the United States.

Finally, you and I must not abandon one another. We must not allow them to make us enemies. Together with Jesus we must walk the road to Jerusalem, unbinding the dead with hope, making the blind to see, freeing women to proclaim the resurrection, curing those men who have been paralyzed by the system and so "have not stood up straight their entire lives."

That is our agenda for 2005. That is the only answer to the new imperialism: We must not, under any circumstances—for the sake of the gospel, for the sake of the world—agree to salute this emperor, whose reign defies the Reign of God.

16.

The Struggle between
Confusion and Expectation

The Legacy of Vatican II

As Vatican II ended, I was just about to begin doctoral studies in
communication theory and social psychology. I didn't know a lot
about either subject at the time but, with one foot in a religious
life spawned by the Council of Trent and the other in a religious
life awash in Vatican II, I knew that anthropologists and social
psychologists were missing the academic news of the century:
Right in front of their eyes, a subculture was about to unleash
its own cultural transformation—by design, with impunity and
in toto. It was a human undertaking of massive proportions. It
added a great deal to religious life but it exacted a cost as well.
Or, as Robert Hooker put it over two centuries ago, "Change
is not made without inconvenience, even from worse to better."

For those who have never experienced the maelstrom of
massive social change, have never lived in the vortex of an institutional storm, have never spent their adult life at the ground
zero of organizational meltdown, it may come as a shock to
realize that "change" and "renewal" are not the same things.
Though Vatican II called the religious orders of the church

to "renewal" it took a great deal of "change" to tap into the marrow of the process. And it is change that can both obstruct and impersonate renewal. In the end, it has been an unending struggle to reconcile the two. The fact is that it is not possible to have renewal without change but it is certainly possible to have change without renewal.

The changes in religious life that had been spurred by Vatican II brought personal maturity, new creativity and transition from the mindset of one century to another. They also brought high expectations, personal confusion, spiritual dis-ease and lack of clarity of purpose.

Maturity, long denied to women religious in the name of obedience, came with relief but not without some angst for women whose entire personal lives had been choreographed by people euphemistically called "superiors." Finally, faced with making decisions common to teenagers—with whom to travel, where to go, what to do, when to be back, how to marshal the resources needed for an event—women religious integrated the two disconnected dimensions of their lives: the personal and the professional. Having been for long years highly developed professionally, they were now able to grow into the kind of adulthood that went with it. They began to make ministry decisions based on personal interests, public needs and particular talents rather than simply on the institutional identities of the congregations to which they belonged. They began to take public positions in non-church institutions—as administrators of welfare centers or soup kitchens or women's shelters, for instance—in order to serve humankind in general, not simply the descendants of the Catholic immigrant population which had prompted their congregation's historic move to this country in the first place. They made public statements, in the manner of any concerned citizen. They took public interest in public situations. They marched in Selma and were arrested in anti-war demonstrations. They moved beyond the denominational to the universal. They grew up and they grew into the world around them. They became a bridge between the strictly spiritual life and an avowedly secular one. They became voices of the gospel in the public arena.

But they also did more than serve established institutions around them. They began to create new ones. They closed old academies to open education centers for the poor. They phased out orphanages to open hospitality houses for the destitute. They formed civil rights groups and began peace and justice centers. Creativity, the right to have new ideas, to suggest new approaches to old problems, to engineer new ways of going about things, to make life new—exhilarating as the possibility may have been—was at the same time, awkward, even frightening for some. Individual religious—whole congregations—quavered between these realities, fixated on the danger of leaning too far, too long, in either one direction or another if the best elements of the past were to be preserved and the most imperative dimensions of the future were to be addressed. Congregations moved in small steps to deal with cosmic questions: They left schools one person at a time, they experimented with schedules one tiny house at a time, they launched new inroads with the new poor, one small soup kitchen at a time, while the rest of the congregation tried to go on attending to the internal questions of new prayer styles, new schedules, new clothes. And one at a time they had to struggle with it. A sister at a parish church with me broke into tears over a run in her hose. Another one got angry because, after fifty years in a convent, she didn't know how to style her hair anymore. A novice set her jaw and said, "I can't wait around here any longer for this to change." Young nuns left religious life in large numbers, disillusioned by the slowness of the small changes and the amount of personal energy that had to be expended over what were to them minuscule issues in apparent danger of never being resolved.

Social transition from the mentality of past centuries to integration into this one—in dress, in ministry, in lifestyle, in personal interactions—took a heavy toll on many. What was really true and permanent, stable and real, if things once defined as permanent, invariable and of the essence of religious life were no longer immutable? The major restructurings Vatican II required in the name of "fidelity to the charism of the founder, the signs of the times, and the needs of the members" broke the hardened shell of religious life into shattered glass.

For many, as a result, religious life as they had lived it was forever over, and with that realization came deep personal despair and a kind of institutional depression. For others, religious life as they envisioned it had only just begun and with that realization came high energy and new commitment to the worthy, the noble, the necessary.

The teeter-totter on which these two elements balance has not completely stabilized yet, a good thirty years after the fact. Nor perhaps should it if the ancient values on which religious life have been based are to fuel the new directions in which it must develop if it is to have anywhere near the social impact of its origins. If the ancient takes over again, religious will be nothing but museum pieces in a surging new world, the dinosaur survivors of a life that is fascinating but irrelevant. If the tradition is lost completely, religious will be nothing but social service workers who make their work their lives. The tension between the two is clearly the very lifeblood of renewal. It was not easy to come by.

The maturity, creativity and social transition of religious of the period were easy to see. More difficult to understand, on the other hand, were the doldrums into which what seemed to be such positive activity was to cast religious life in general. After years of membership loss, especially among the newer, younger members of congregations who were disaffected by the control and routinization of a life they had expected to find charismatic or prophetic, even fewer women entered a developing Vatican II religious life, whatever its new directions and its new developments. The question in the face of the new creativity, the clear maturity and the necessary social transition was why? The answers may well be many. But there are at least two, which, in the climate of the time may well deserve consideration. In the first place, the Catholic population itself, whatever its deepest attitudes toward Vatican I religious life, was not prepared for the changes sparked by Vatican II. In the second place, religious communities themselves, though awash in change, had yet to be able to ground change in renewal.

Vatican II was an event whose hour did not really come. Most pastors, formed in another council themselves, gave few homilies on the subject and provided even fewer programs. Lay people were left to cope with change altar rail by altar rail, hymn by hymn, liturgy by liturgy. There were few explanations given, little theology taught. Parishes simply implemented new formulas, accepted nuns in new habits—grudgingly in many places—said prayers in new translations and watched in sullen sadness or deep resentment as the church as they had known it faded into oblivion.

Of all the church, the people most mobilized for change were women religious. Mandated to hold renewal chapters and write renewal constitutions, groups retrained their entire memberships in the theology of Vatican II in anticipation of what would of necessity be a community project. Change was impossible without the support of the entire group. The work moved quickly. Groups suspended their Vatican I constitutions and instituted experimentation in every area of religious life. The work moved quickly, but almost entirely internally. There was very little consciousness of the confusion it generated among a laity that had no idea whatsoever why the changes in process were historically sound, let alone necessary, and even less rehearsal for it.

It was an exciting time. It was also a dangerous time, a time of great personal tension and deep spiritual struggle. Religious themselves asked, Why stay when life here was just like life anywhere else? Why give up so much for nothing? Lay women and religious themselves asked, Why give yourself to a life so unlike any other if, in the end, they were all the same? No "higher" vocations? No hundredfold? No privilege or special treatment or public status? It was a question that begged for answers. It was the renewal question that no amount of change could supply.

The truth is that religious had been formed in the spirituality of the virgins and martyrs, of sacrifice and perseverance—virtues men had traditionally required of women—when what Vatican II called for was the spirituality of priests and prophets, of community building and witness. It was, then, on the deepening, the broadening, of both personal development and spirituality that the transition to Vatican II religious life really depended. To bring the church into the modern world, it would take a spirituality far beyond docility and childlike obedience. It would take women of commitment to life and courage for the unknown. But prophecy and risk are not the hallmarks of large groups. It is not large groups that started religious life and it is not large groups that will renew it now. Religious life must travel light into the future, burdened by nothing of its successes of the past, held down by none of its past goals but fresh in direction, vital in its meanings for the people of today.

A movement that loses its radical creative edge loses its vision and its reason for existence. A movement that is only radical loses its popular base and its stabilizing foundation. The continuing task of Vatican II is to sharpen the edge of religious life again. What religious did for past generations, they must now do for those forgotten peoples of our own generation. A whole new global population must be carried beyond the limitations of their lives, become visible to those who see them not, be heard by those who are deaf to their tears.

The truth is that out of this conflict between creativity and spiritual confusion has come something far more dynamic than either. The image of a religious life steeped in the prophetic dimensions of its founders and at the same time deeply immersed in the life of the spirit, the search for the holy, and the spiritual wisdom of the past is becoming ever more apparent. Lay people by the thousands are attaching themselves to the prayer life and ministry of women religious, who have found their old identity again in new ways. Associate, oblate, and lay membership programs are thriving. Women's centers and retreat programs are developing out of women's congregations all over the country. Women are entering religious life again: older now, yes, but totally committed in whole new ways to doing the new things that the new suffering need; they are being educated, formed and directed by women's congregations everywhere. More than that, religious communities are beginning to realize that everyone who comes to a religious community does not want to stay forever, a principle of membership understood and integrated by Buddhist monasteries for thousands of years. Now, temporary membership is a developing dimension of religious life in a culture where few expect to do anything forever anymore.

Conformity is no longer the major religious virtue, togetherness masking as community, and the fear of change is no longer the agenda of religious life. Renewal of spirit, openness to new needs and depth, if not necessarily length, of personal commitment has become the new norm. "Why did you come here?" I asked a new applicant. "Because this is the only group of women I have been able to find that cares about exactly what I do—community, the gospel of Jesus, and a commitment to peace and justice," she said simply. Interestingly enough, I couldn't help but think that her answer sounded to me exactly like what Vatican II wanted from religious, too: that they would examine their life from the perspective of the "charism of the founder, the needs of society, and the gifts of their members." But, if that's the case, religious life is not only new again, it is also a long way from being over.

17.

Fasting

If Ireland is a bellwether of anything today, it is surely of the Catholic consciousness. The Angelus still plays on public TV and radio at noon and 6:00 p.m. every day. Stations—house Masses that developed during penal times when the practice of Catholicism was forbidden by British law—are still practiced in rural areas. St. Brigid's Day is even more of a celebration in some ways here than St. Patrick's Day.

But don't be deceived. All is not traditional anymore. When the waitress took our orders in the little village restaurant in the west of Ireland, for instance, she didn't know how to respond to my request that the chef wrap a starter of goat cheese in something besides ham. "The meat," I explained. "It's Lent." She looked more puzzled, raised her eyebrows, and scurried away from the table, confused and embarrassed.

I was in Ireland in Lent 2006 and the Friday fast meant absolutely nothing. And why was I surprised?

"The Challenge of Peace," the 1983 peace pastoral of the US bishops' conference, called on Catholics to return to the Friday fast as an act of penance for peace. They wrote: "We call upon our people voluntarily to do penance on Friday by eating less food and by abstaining from meat. This return to a traditional practice of penance, once well observed in the US Church, should be accompanied by works of charity and service toward our neighbors. Every Friday should be a day significantly devoted to prayer, penance, and almsgiving for peace."

Almost no one I know is doing it. The question is: Should we? And if we should, why aren't we?

Fasting had a greater effect on me in my childhood than something as significant as "trans-sub-stan-ti-a-tion." Transubstantiation, they told me, was the changing of the bread and wine into the Body and Blood of Christ. But that I took for granted. Fasting, on the other hand, this foreign way of going about life, was something that called for real change in the way I lived.

In the Eucharist, Jesus changed for my sake. In fasting, I was being called to change for something far beyond my own sake. Fasting made a kind of demand on me that few other things ever did.

What it was and why anyone would do it became an even more important question as the years went by. Most of all, if the practice of fasting was so good, why had it disappeared?

When a practice strays far from its original intentions, it often must disappear so that it can be rediscovered for the right reasons. Fasting is certainly one of those practices.

I remember as a youngster dining in a convent during Lent and being curious about the small set of brass scales between every four place settings. "That's for weighing our food during Lent," the nun showing us the house explained.

Years later I entered a monastery myself. But there were no scales on the tables. The Rule of Benedict taught that we were to fast during Lent, true, but added that we were also to "add to the usual measure of our service something by way of private prayer" and "holy reading and almsgiving."

Now there was a twist. Clearly fasting was about something more than simple deprivation. Obviously fasting was supposed to add something to our lives as well as to take something away.

It was meant to sensitize us to life more than it was to deprive us of it.

But when not fasting was no longer defined as a "mortal sin," it disappeared overnight. Fasting for my generation became more burden than blessing, more an attempt to punish the body than an invitation to strengthen the soul. We managed to concentrate on beating the body down rather than showing the value of emptying ourselves of clutter so we could concentrate on something besides ourselves.

Fasting over the centuries became a kind of mathematical legerdemain of the soul. Meals had times, lengths and quantities attached to them. The scales kept portions under four ounces; the distinction between juices and soups and solids kept us paranoid about the differences between them. If heaven and hell depend on it, a person can get very nervous. No wonder modern psychology found fasting suspect. It had lost all semblance of sense for the heart or gift for the soul.

When Vatican II came along with its emphasis more on spirit than rules, people put down some rules immediately. Fasting, for obvious reasons, was one of them.

But the practice of fasting cannot be easily dismissed. Fasting is the unfinished chapter in post–Vatican II spirituality because the reasons for it abound.

The place of fasting in the lives of all the great spiritual figures in history brings no small amount of weight to the subject. Time, too, recommends we revisit the subject, as fasting has been a constant tradition in the church for twenty centuries. Finally, the presence of fasting in all spiritual traditions, not just Catholicism, makes a person pause. In all places and times, fasting has been a hallmark of the person on a serious search for the spiritual dimensions of life.

How do we explain the meaning of fasting in our own times? The answers ring with the kind of simplicity and depth common only to the holiest of disciplines. The fact is that the values of fasting strike to the heart of a person, sharpen the soul to the presence of God, and energize the spirit in a way engorgement never can.

Fasting calls a person to authenticity. It empties us, literally, of all the non-essentials in our lives so we have room for God. It lifts our spirits beyond the mundane.

Fasting confronts our consumer mentality with a reminder of what it is to be dependent on God. It reminds us that we are not here simply to pamper ourselves. We are, indeed, expected to be our brother and sister's keeper. We know why we are hungry. We voluntarily gave up the food we could have had. But why are they hungry? Where is the food they should be eating? And what can we do to fill them now that we are done filling only ourselves?

Fasting opens us to the truth. It makes space in us to hear others, to ask the right questions, to ingest the answers we have been too comfortable to care about for far too long. It makes room for adding "to our service a bit more prayer and reading and almsgiving," as the Rule of Benedict says.

Fasting requires us to develop a sense of limits. No, we may not have it all, do it all, and demand it all. Our needs do not exceed the needs of others, and our needs may never become more important than theirs.

Fasting teaches us to say no to ourselves in small things so that we may have the strength to say no to those people and systems and governments who want to use us to shore up their own power and profit despite the needs of others.

When we fast, we become voluntarily poor and so understand the needs of the poor. When we fast, we say yes to the Spirit and no to the lusts within us that drive us to live for money and power and profit and the kind of engorgement that renders the rest of the world destitute.

No doubt about it: Fasting surely has something to do with peacemaking. It puts us in touch with the Creator. It puts us in touch with ourselves. It puts us in touch with the prophet Jesus who, fasting in the desert, gave up power, wealth, comfort and self-centeredness, and teaches us to do the same. It puts us in touch with the rest of the creation whose needs now cry out in our own.

18.

Seeds of a New Humanity

The mystic Julian of Norwich, holding a hazelnut in her hand in the fourteenth century, said of it, "In this is all that is." The earth shakes at the thought of the simple truth of it.

In every seed lie the components of all life the world has known from all time to now. In every seed is the reckless, electric, confounding power of creation made new again. In every seed is the gift of life to those seeking life, wanting life, denied the kind of life that is full of energy, full of hope.

But the hope is a tenuous one, a sacred one, one to be treated with awe for fear of our own failures to protect it.

Seeds are the one thing that is the only genuine promise we have of the future. "Even if I knew the world would end tomorrow," Martin Luther wrote, "I would plant an apple tree today." It is an insight that defies despair, that promises new life in the midst of the old. It is a beacon that cries out for commitment in an age such as ours when the seeds of destruction among us—greed, power, control—are in mortal struggle with the seeds of life.

In our time, death is king. The forests die for the sake of loggers. Great fish die for the sake of caviar. The fields die for the sake of fracking. The air dies for the sake of oil. Humanity dies for the sake of money. And people die for want of the food that all these things threaten.

And now, so accustomed have we become to destruction in the name of progress, we are on the brink of commercializing seed, of politicizing seed, of monopolizing seed, of genetically modifying seed for the sake of someone's control of creation, of making seed the new military weapon of the twenty-first century.

It is all a matter of valuing the money we can make today more than we value the life that is meant to come.

But the problem is that we ourselves are all seeds, too. We are either seeds of universal love or seeds of exploitative racism. We are seeds of eternal hope or we are seeds of starving despair. We are seeds of a new humanity or we are the harbingers of humanity's decay.

It is a choice. A conscious choice that depends on what we see in seeds and how we treat them and whose we think they are and what we will do to keep them free and available. Or not.

We are the seed of our own life to come and the life of the planet as well. Indeed, "In the seed is everything that is."

19.

Stages in the Spiritual Life

The spiritual life is not a template; it is a process meant to change our lives. There are stages in the spiritual life that move us from one level to another.

The first is compliance. The Ten Commandments dominate in this phase. Being spiritual in this phase depends on keeping a list of dos and don'ts, on keeping the "rules"—whatever they are—on being perfect.

This kind of spiritual score keeping is a necessary but very immature stage. We concern ourselves with actions rather than attitudes. We worry about not insulting someone, perhaps, but not about wanting to insult them.

The point is that we don't make choices in this stage. Not real choices. We simply conform or rebel. We do what we're told and call ourselves holy for having done so. We do everything we're told but we never ask ourselves whether or not what we're doing has anything at all to do with the Beatitudes or not.

The second level of the spiritual life is awareness. It has more to do with becoming Christian than it does with going through the rituals of being Christian. This stage of spiritual development awakens in us the awareness that our role as Christians is to help make the world a just and peaceful place. We are not here simply to make ourselves paragons of organizational piety.

At the second level of the spiritual life, we come to realize that though God began the process of Creation it is our responsibility to complete it. Then we set out to become the kind of people we were put on earth to be. We begin to go out of ourselves for the sake of the world rather than simply awarding ourselves gold stars for being regular observers of ancient rituals. "Do not wish to be called holy before you are holy," the desert monastics taught. It is holiness, not regularity, that we are now about in our spiritual life.

Finally, the third level of the spiritual life is transformation. It requires that we ourselves begin to "put on the mind of Christ." We ourselves begin to think like Jesus of the Mount of Beatitudes who in the face of the Ten Commandments required love that was demanding, holier than laws could ever be. We face what it means to be just in an unjust world, meek in an arrogant one, humble in a domineering one, compassionate in a prejudiced one, full of grief for those who suffer from suffering not of their own doing, compassionate for those who are oppressed by the indifferent of this world.

Then the truly spiritual soul sees the world as God sees the world and sets out to make it right. But that can happen only if we spend our lives immersed in the scripture, steeped in its passion for good, conscious of its struggles, in tune with the heart of God.

PART III

EVER ANCIENT, EVER NEW:
THE MONASTIC VISION

Introduction

Is to be Benedictine enough for us here in this place and now at this time? Or are we, in this era, intent on being Benedictine enough to launch this tradition into the process of saving Western civilization for another fifteen hundred years? These questions are the essence of Benedictinism. The answers are totally ours.

—JOAN CHITTISTER

For fifteen hundred years Pax/Peace has been the bedrock of Benedictine monasticism. For fifteen hundred years the Rule of Benedict has offered succeeding periods of history values that could uphold peaceful societies. As Sister Joan writes, such values include "common ownership of goods, equality of status, the common life, reception of the stranger, simplicity of life, care of the environment and ongoing conversion of life."

For fifteen hundred years vowed Benedictine women and men have embodied these values in changing historical eras. Whether through the reformist vision of a Hildegard of Bingen or the artistic vision of a Brother Thomas Bezanson, time and time again Benedictine monasticism has remained faithful to these values. In every era, culture and circumstance in which a monastery finds itself, reading "the signs of the times" becomes the clear and constant call for monastics.

For fifteen hundred years, despite fluctuation of membership, lack of ecclesial support, fear of the unknown, and the ever-constant need for institutional updating and change, Benedictine communities have faced each era and the future determined

167

to prevail in bringing Jesus' vision of the Reign of God to the world.

Thus, Sister Joan insists, "Without doubt, the world in which we live now needs, as it did in Benedict's time, reflection, conscience, spiritual development, human service, equality, ecumenical interaction and social critique. To be seen as significant enough to attract others to such a life, Benedictines must spend their own lives to make it real."

Succinctly, then, she heralds *Succisa virescit*: "Cut down, it ever grows again."

—MARY HEMBROW SNYDER

20.

St. Benedict of Nursia, Benedictine Monasticism and Peace

What is known about Benedict of Nursia, the founder of Western monasticism, is scant. What is known about the effects of his Rule on the development of Western civilization is not. In fact, those data reach back fifteen hundred years and touch the educational, economic and social dimensions of every country in Europe and eventually much of the rest of the Western world as well.

Benedict of Nursia was born in Italy in AD 480 during a period of major social upheaval and studied in a Rome that was decadent and declining. Tribal invaders from the north and east had overrun the borders and provinces of the Empire in every direction. Rome had been sacked by Alaric and the Huns in 410 and again in 455 by the Vandals. In 476, the foreigner Odoacer had deposed the boy-emperor Romulus. Struggle for the control of the west became a constant. Control was impossible, governance was weak, the economy was disrupted, and the people were powerless. Europe became a battleground for political power and profit for centuries.

In the face of such corruption, Benedict of Nursia left Rome to become a hermit at Subiaco, a deserted region some forty miles away. His fame as a holy person grew and before long followers gathered around him for counsel and direction. With them and the social situation in mind, Benedict developed a new style of life and wrote his Rule for monastics.

To the disordered environment of the time, monasticism brought stability, organizational effectiveness, and spiritual values. The Rule which Benedict wrote in the face of such cultural cataclysm stood in direct repudiation of the social concepts common at that time.

In the face of a government that valued hierarchy, Benedict designed a community of equals: the educated and illiterate, the noble and the slave all lived side by side bound by the same laws and living the same lifestyle.

In the face of unmitigated attempts at power, control and wealth, Benedict prescribed common ownership and outlawed the appropriation of goods for personal gain.

In the face of a class system based both on wealth and lineage, Benedict insisted on humility and mutual obedience.

In the face of human oppression and manipulation, Benedict outlawed slavery and insisted on manual labor for all.

In the face of competition, coercion and class struggle, Benedict insisted on peace, within self and with others, with community members and strangers alike.

The principles of Benedictine monasticism spread quickly. Consequently, the new and powerful barbarian tribes were converted to the principles of Christianity by these monastics who did not eschew work, and monasteries became the social, educational and spiritual centers of the new society. From them, creative works of agriculture, conservation, reforestation, education and hospitality brought order and productivity to what with the fall of the Roman Empire had been a basically shattered social situation. Benedictine nuns and monks grew in public prominence and influence. Peace was the cornerstone of the monastic values, the inscription over monastery portals, the ideal of the life.

Monasteries were the prime transmitters of the pacifist tradition. As radical Christians, monastics did not engage in warfare. Chrysostom described pacifism as essential to the monastic vocation. He wrote: "If you consider war, then the monk fights with demons and having conquered is crowned by Christ. Kings fight with barbarians. Inasmuch as demons are more fearful than barbarians, the victory of the monks is more glorious. The monk fights for the religion and true worship of God . . . the king to capture booty, being inspired by envy and the lust of power" (Migne). The gospel mandate, "Thou shalt not kill" was a law not to be mitigated in the name of nationalism (Matthew 5:21–26; see also Exodus 20:13 and 21:12; Deuteronomy 5:17). Monasteries, in fact, became sanctuaries for those fleeing the ravages of feudal war, arbitrators of local disputes and keepers of the peace. Ecclesiastical attempts at social order and protection in the eleventh century such as the Peace of God and the Truce of God, which were cultural movements and pacts created to assure peace or at least to guarantee periods of suspension of hostilities, were rooted in the monasteries of the time.

The monasteries, in other words, did not exist only for the sake of the monastics attached to them. But the warfare they waged in the name of protection was quite unlike the chivalric or feudal codes of the men of the society around them. The ancient Rule reads: "To you, therefore, my speech is now directed, who, giving up your own will, take up the strong and most excellent arms of obedience, to do battle for Christ the Lord, the true King" (RB, Prologue, par. 2). The battle was for the Christian life and conversion of souls. Peace was the monk's "quest and aim" (RB, Prologue, 1.17).

To this day, the qualities basic to the Rule of Benedict form the foundation for the peaceful society. Benedictine life requires common ownership of goods, equality of status, the common life, reception of the stranger, simplicity of life, care of the environment and ongoing conversion of life. Peace with self through prayer, peace with others in hospitality, peace with the earth through work and peace within community through mutual obedience provide the model for human relationships. Rampant nationalism, classism and domination are all put to rout in the face of a community of strangers who put down their differences and private ambitions to become a sign of human family.

In the nuclear period, the Benedictine consciousness of its heritage of peace is reaching new proportions. In the United States the national organization Benedictines for Peace, in direct response to the historical charism of the Order, became the first association to create a federation of religious committed to nuclear disarmament, and the international Benedictine Confederation declared in its 1984 Congress of Abbots its continuing concern for the issue.

21.

Vows

The concept of vow is an ancient one. The Old Testament speaks often of the offering to God of objects, persons or the self as promises made consciously and voluntarily to perform good works (Nm 15:1–10; Lv 27). Though vows were not required of the pious Jew, once made they were to be carried out with precision and rigor (Dt 23:22–24).

Nazirites were those Israelites who consecrated themselves to the service of God in specific ways for limited periods of time or for life (Nm 6:1–8). Though abuses concerning vows were common and denounced by the prophets, nevertheless the practice of taking vows was not repudiated by the early church and, in fact, remained a time-honored one that continued to be common. Paul himself, on his last journey to Jerusalem, took a temporary Nazirite vow (Acts 21:22–26).

Monastic life in the early Christian tradition was also based on a commitment to renunciation and virginity. Monastics of the fourth and fifth centuries, though not bound by formal, public vows, committed themselves to virginity and life according to a specific rule. Furthermore, both the Greek Fathers of the Church (Origen and Gregory of Nyssa) and the Latin Fathers of the Church (Cyprian and Augustine) recognized the validity of solemn promises made to God and the sacred obligations they incurred.

The vow, in other words, consists of a public commitment to do a specified good for the sake of religious dedication or "divine service," the giving of the self to God. It is both a public contract and a public witness, the value of which does not lie in choosing good over bad in life but in choosing good above good. To vow poverty, for instance, is not to despise the goods of creation but to commit oneself to dependence on God and the just distribution of the goods of the earth in order to be free from the burdens that come with the amassment of wealth and which may distract a person from the development of the spiritual realities of life. A person does not take the vow of virginity because sexual expression is bad but because the control of passion and total consecration to God in the spiritual life is itself a good. The vow of obedience is not designed to curb human decision-making, the supreme act of humanity, but to point to the presence and demands of a Law above human law.

Though this type of obliging dedication was assumed from the time of the earliest monastic groups, the term "vow" itself comes later upon the scene. The Latin concept of *propositum* or "promise," the Spanish term *pactum* or "contract" and St. Basil's *homologia* or "commitment" all connoted a vocational decision to the monastery but not a matter of ecclesiastical contract. This desire to serve God in a particular monastery by following a specific rule, then, is a form of commitment that promises in public a pledge of fidelity to a given way of life in a given group. In its earliest understandings, however, these commitments were not seen as public promises to fulfill a public pious act for the sake of a greater good in quite the same spirit that characterized the vows made in the Hebrew scriptures.

As time went on, however, and religious life took on a more formal character in the church, the understanding of commitment itself changed.

Since the choice of a lifestyle—marriage or religious life—is a social act with ramifications for the rest of society, its public declaration is both significant and customary. These obligations to God, in other words, affect a person's relationship to humankind as well. Consequently, society has a right to call the vowed person to accountability and has a corresponding responsibility to support them since, in binding themselves to the service of God, they bind themselves in a special way, too, to the needs of humanity. A public vow, therefore, is a public gift to the church which the church through an official agency recognizes, accepts and affirms in an equally public fashion by receiving the vow and authorizing the compact.

The theology of vows that is developed by Thomas Aquinas is reiterated and emphasized in the rebuttal of the Council of Trent to the position of the Protestant reformers that vows are contrary to the nature of Baptism. This Tridentine theology of the vows stressed individual asceticism and withdrawal from the secular world. The Vatican II theology of the vows, on the other hand, rejects the dualism of the eighteenth century for the sake of a more Trinitarian and communal notion of the vowed life and its role in society.

The chief witness value of religious vows lies in the fact that vows promise the future of the individual as well as the present. Vows, in other words, are more than isolated good works done under a particular set of circumstances. Vows oblige the person to long-term dedication to a specific good. Vows are, then, public acts of faith in the eternal goodness and fidelity of God. Though they may be commuted under special circumstances and for special reasons or even taken for temporary periods of time, the vows of religious life are normally taken for a lifetime.

This conscious commitment to a lifetime effort and single-minded dedication make for constancy in times of whim or stress if for no other reason than the seriousness with which they have been taken and the public dimension of their character. Not taken lightly, vows are not normally dismissed lightly.

Vows, then, differ from precepts because they promise more than moral law obliges. They give perpetual emphasis, strength and embodiment to a particular facet, or counsels, of the Christian life. Everyone is to live with the poor in mind, of course, but those who take a vow of poverty bind themselves to make that quality present in the church. Everyone, married or single, is to live chastely according to their state in life but the vow of chastity obliges the religious to attest to the fact that chastity and celibacy are possible. Everyone is to obey the gospel mandate but the vow of obedience requires the religious to put the law of the gospel above every other law in life.

Precepts command but they do not oblige under law. The counsels are based on the life of Christ but differ from the commandments or the vows in that they are spiritual directives but not legal prescripts. The vows, unlike either precepts or counsels, have an expectation of the fulfillment of specific conditions, can only be dispensed by the proper authority and take on a public responsibility to a greater good.

Vows signal the total giving over of one's life to the God of history as well as of eternity in order to live in the image of Christ and bring the kingdom of God. The vows, in other words, are not signs of what life is to be in another world but of what life can be in this one.

22.

Old Vision
for a New Age

The story of Monte Cassino and its Coat of Arms touches every Benedictine heart. "*Succisa virescit*"—Cut down, it ever grows again—we remind ourselves interminably. *Succisa virescit* as the novitiates empty. *Succisa virescit* as monasteries merge. *Succisa virescit* as the number of members everywhere shrivels to half the volume of the last thirty years. *Succisa virescit* we say as the world changes around us and we change very little at all.

Clearly the question we need to ask is whether, in our complacent assurance of eternal institutional life, we are living in myth or in reality. Reality, if we are willing to face it, can teach us things about growth. Myth, on the other hand, if we take it literally rather than seriously, may simply drive us, like lemmings on the way to the sea, to our own destruction.

The point is not whether or not monasticism is renewable. Hundreds of years of history tell us that it is. It is obviously not unreal, then, to expect a monastery to be able to negotiate change as well as multiple other social institutions around it do. The point is whether or not we are willing to renew it. The number of now extinct communities tells us that to expect renewal without being willing to pay its price is sheer myth.

The question of renewal is, in other words, not philosophical alone. It is psychological as well. To change an institution in which we have been formed, of which we have no other image, requires more than fidelity; it requires the emotional maturity and the living faith to believe that the vision that spawned it lives on even after the structures which expressed it are in need of replacement.

We search everywhere for the kind of answers that can possibly explain the present moment to ourselves in ways that make future directions clear as well. Why the loss of membership? Why the apparent loss of public interest in an institution that has, over and over again, been its mainstay, its avant garde in a shifting universe of change? It is Benedictines who honed the educational system, saved the manuscripts of Europe, created a hospice system for travelers, developed a welfare system for the poor, were the judges, the teachers, the agronomists of the time. And they did all of it out of a vision shaped daily, hourly, by the call of the prophets and the image of Jesus. So what can possibly be the problem?

We have some favorite shibboleths to explain our own situation, of course. It's not that the answers we give ourselves are not plausible. It is simply that they are not as defensible as they may appear at first glance.

In a highly secularized world, religion has lost its impact, we say. But religion has never been more prominent in world culture than it is right now. In fact, religious fundamentalists from the center of the United States to the center of the globe are fighting fierce culture wars to save the soul of the system as they see it.

The world breeds materialism, we say, and families no longer encourage their young into altruistic or low-paying vocations. But the Peace Corps, the Greens, international aid programs and social volunteerism have never been higher. The truth is that the one great life choice to which young people are not giving their lives is religious life.

It's just a bad period, we say. We just need to go on doing what we've always done until this period is over and things will be normal again. But this "period" is already almost fifty years in the making and not only are the signs of growth not getting better, they are, by and large, getting worse. Nor do we ask what "normal" is supposed to be for those who claim to be following the Jesus who walked from Galilee to Jerusalem curing the sick, raising the dead, feeding the hungry.

The image of ostriches comes far too readily to mind.

One thing we seldom do is to look for the answer to the present situation in ourselves rather than in the world around us. What is it, in a lifestyle we love, that fails to communicate itself to the world around it?

Or does it?

The fact is that people young and old, married and unmarried, flock to our monasteries even now, even yet. They come for retreats, for programs, for prayer and for community projects. They help us in our works, contribute to our existence, join our activities and revere our elderly. But they do not come to stay. Clearly the purpose of the monastic lifestyle as lifestyle simply does not appeal to them, lacks meaning to them, fails to engage them in the great human enterprise of the spiritual life. What they hear when they get to our monasteries does not magnetize them, does not keep them, does not draw them into the effort itself. It does not excite their hearts enough to make staying worthwhile. But it is only purpose now, not the old self-aggrandizement of salvation, not the fear of hell that can possibly enthrall them.

The situation reeks of the most frustrating kind of simplicity: Monasticism is obviously in transition. Some, if numbers mean anything, would say declining, in fact. Over fifteen hundred years of history, however, give no small witness to the fact that monasticism is a hardy but flexible institution that has weathered age after age. Other major lifestyle forms, both secular and religious, have disappeared forever in even less amount of time—

the Knights Templar, the Shakers, the feudal system, Puritanism among them—but not Benedictine monasticism.

If any group ought to be able to translate from one moment in history to another, then surely monasticism would seem likely to be one of them. Even more convincing, perhaps, is that, with the exception of Judaism, for which family life is taken to a divine mandate—all major religious traditions—Hinduism, Buddhism, and Islam—have nurtured the image of the single-minded seeker of the Divine for whom communal life was an important part of the search. Serious researchers even presume that as human beings we are as wired for religion as we are wired for language, in which case it is, it seems, part of the human condition for some people to give their lives to the search for the ultimate in life.

Add to that the stirrings of religious revival generated by a world at war in the last century and it is not surprising to see that Benedictine monasticism which had withered under the anti-religious, anti-Catholic movements of nineteenth-century Europe flowered again in the twentieth. Monasteries grew in membership. More than 250 foundations took root in areas outside the Western world. Schools and colleges everywhere flourished.

What seemed like a new flowering of monasticism did not last five hundred to one thousand years this time, however. Nothing does anymore. Communication is too continual; ferment is too persistent; change is too constant. Now, it is stability of purpose, not stability of systems that counts as the world shifts around us. And shift it did.

By the mid-twentieth century, the whole world was embroiled in an even more impacting kind of social cataclysm. Technology, social mobility, feminism, globalism, scientific advancement at unheard of rates, space travel, individualism, the sexual revolution and an ecumenical council that opened the church itself to critical re-evaluation turned the world and its long-standing assumptions upside down.

It was a time of unparalleled newness. The convergence of science, democracy, social consciousness, technology and theologies of liberation swept away just as many systems in their wake as the world up to now had taken for granted. With them went all the social absolutes upon which the whole Western system had been based: that women were secondary creatures, for instance, that people of color were less than fully human, that nation states were inviolable, that the US-European West was the center of the universe, that Catholicism was the only major religion on earth.

New ways of living and being alive, new ways of relating to one another, new horizons in the face of the breakdown of bygone boundaries unleashed new social systems and led to the reexamination of old ones. The new world began to eclipse the past, to bring it into question, to smother it. Only the memories of those who yearned for the older, more stable, more secure, less challenging world preserved it. Only the memories—and in their midst the question that emerged in the shadow of them: What was monasticism really supposed to be?

It was the beginning of a new moment in time, not all of it good but all of it powerful. The twentieth century was a crossover point in history at least as major as the rise of nationalism in the thirteenth century, the discovery of the New World in the fifteenth century, the religious reformation in the sixteenth century, the scientific revolutions of the seventeenth century and the democratic revolutions of the eighteenth century,

Every major institution felt the shock waves of it all: marriage, government, economics, and, of course, religion.

God, in a period of quantum physics and space travel, became an idea to be clung to passionately or an idol to be destroyed. God was not dead anymore; God was irrelevant—a state far worse than the first.

Women discovered their abilities and claimed their personhood as moral agents, as full members of the human race, as shapers of every dimension of it. White men discovered their limitations and strained to understand what it means to be simply equal members of the human race, not definers of it. Couples struggled to discover new ways of being together that did not depend on the invisibility of one for the sake of the other.

Young people—both young men and young women—had a world to explore. Gone were the days of limited roles and narrow options. New possibilities opened for them from one end of the globe to another. Women could be pilots; men could be nurses; women could be executives; men could be stay-at-home-husbands. Options became the name of the game.

Science had a world to create, animals to clone, birth to alter, life and death to reconfigure. The clash of consciousness that such meteoric and total reinterpretations of what had, for generations, been seen as immutable human processes might create for society as a whole never entered the picture. What Marshall McLuhan had once named "culture shock"—the inability of a group to absorb the meaning of rapid change—became a commonplace of the human condition.

Business had a world to rape and ravage for its own profit, whatever cost to anyone anywhere, and in the doing of it, changed the lives of peoples and villages and countries from one point of the globe to the next.

Technology had at its fingertips now a whole world to connect and engage in great common questions, in new global works. Satellite towers went up in Peoria and Peru, in Kentucky and Kenya, in Appalachia and Afghanistan. Technology made international voyeurs of us all. We could no longer plead that we didn't know, didn't see, didn't have anything to do with the poverty, the oppression, the impossible life situations which our lifestyle had imposed on others. The "world village" had come home to us all with a vengeance. None of us were innocent anymore.

This was not the world of Benedict of Nursia. Or anything close to it.

And yet in the world of Benedict of Nursia there is surely a model, a vision, of what must be done to exist in a world such as this one. The Benedictinism that stabilized Europe, that gave a center to its villages and a spiritual glue to its systems, has never been needed more.

The problem is that those of us who now carry the ideals of the last century into this one straddle both of those worlds. We have one foot in a formation model that was local, agrarian and hierarchical. We have the other foot in a global, urban, techno-logical, science-centered democratic world in flux.

The question with which such a situation faces us as we try to foresee the future of monasticism, to recommit ourselves to its lasting vision, is a major one, a fundamental one, a dangerous one. And it is all the more dangerous because it is so basic and the answer is so simple. What becomes of monasticism in such a shifting universe, now and in the immediate future, depends on how this generation understands the essential purpose and nature of monasticism itself.

It is not how we pass judgment on the nature and character of the world around us that will determine whether or not mo-nasticism can once again be a vital force in a world that often confuses the practice of religion with the soul of religion. It is how we see ourselves functioning in that world that will make the difference.

The question that confronts our time is very much the one that confronted Benedict himself: What exactly is "the contem-plative life"?

The answer to this, and the vision of monasticism that de-velops out of it, depends on whether or not contemplation is described as an active or a passive dimension of the spiritual life.

If we understand contemplation to be the energy that drives us out of ourselves, into the mind of God and from there into a world waiting for the Word, we will have one vision of the monastic life.

If, on the other hand, we define contemplation as the magnet that draws us away from the questions of this life, into space unsullied by "the world," we will have another perspective on monasticism.

Whichever we choose—immersion or distance, transcendence or transformation, incarnation or intellection—will determine the nature of the communities in which we live.

History has not always benefited the discussion. The tendency over time has been to make the terms "contemplative" and "cloister" synonymous—as if place were the determining factor in the making of a contemplative, as if Jesus was not a "contemplative," as if all of us are not called to be "contemplative." As a result, where we did what we did came to be more important than what we did and who we cared for and what we said and to whom we said it. In fact, it circumscribed life to the point that there were boundaries to what we could and could not see, could and could not address. We came from a contemplative tradition and arrested the process of our contemplation in mid-flight.

But not all. Some of our most contemplative figures—Catherine of Siena, Thomas Merton, Hildegard of Bingen—have been our most active. Some of our most active figures—Teresa of Avila, Dorothy Day, Ignatius of Loyola—have been our most contemplative.

If the contemplative, then, is the one who comes to see the world as God sees the world, the one who puts on the mind of Christ for the world, the one who cries out the will of God for the world, in the cloister and out of it, out of it as well as in it, then the vision of monastic life changes radically.

A basic principle of group formation is that every group attracts what it is. If we ourselves are passive in a world that cries out for both the spiritual life and the redemption it brings to the sordid and the unholy, then we will attract the passive. If we ourselves cry out loud with the prophets for the redemption of the world around us, then our prayer is true and our contemplation is real and the monasticism we live is a firebrand in the midst of the world.

It is that vision of monasticism, the monasticism that saved Europe, that brought peace and order, yes, but brought challenge and voice, as well—to the sick on the sides of the road, to the poor in the fields, to the illiterate in the streets, to the oppressed in the cities, to the dispossessed on the highways and to the unemployed in its villages. This is the Benedictinism that reforested Europe, reclaimed its swamp lands and made rules to keep the Peace of God in the midst of its wars, employed the serfs, taught their children and housed their sick. This is the Benedictinism that came out of the cave to attend to the shepherds in the fields.

That is the Benedictinism that young people and old are waiting to see again in us, to hear again from us, to live again with us if Benedictinism is to save the best of this world and, at the same time, give witness to the new world that they are waiting to see here and now among them.

The monastic community, historically a center of life and stability in a reeling world, exists to provide a vision of a new world lived in harmony—with one another, with the community of nations, and with the planet. It is not Rome, now, that needs to be confronted with a clear, prophetic voice of justice and peace. It is Washington, the World Bank, the IMF. It is sexism, racism, clericalism and materialism that are strangling the life out of people. It is elitism, militarism and nuclearism that are really terrorizing the world. And it is Benedictinism with its accents on a community of equals, the common voice, stewardship, peace, individual needs, Sabbath, work, openness to the world, and immersion in the mind of God that has the language for it.

In order to meet that potential in this age, when the world is steeped in social chaos, economic uncertainty, international tension, institutionalized injustice, secularism, sexism and the sense of futility that comes with a feeling of powerlessness in the face of major forces, monastic communities must become signs of hope.

Monastic communities of the future need to give new meaning and bold shape to whole new ways of being a public voice in a world deafened by the social bedlam in which it exists.

To be a living model of the scriptural foundation of the Rule of Benedict, monastic communities must begin to develop new ways of addressing these new issues rather than simply ignoring them. The painful truth is that by ignoring them, we perpetuate them in the name of having removed ourselves from responsibility for them by virtue of the contemplative dimension of our lives. Worse, by ignoring them, we identify ourselves with them by our silence in the face of them.

On the contrary. To be a new voice in the world again, to be a new model of Benedictine life in a new world, a new vision of the Christian life in the world today, monastic communities must devise new methods of outreach, new ways of sharing the fruits of their contemplation with the world around them. The tools and skills, the insights and professional expertise to deal with each are already alive within us and our monastic communities. It is simply a matter of doing consciously and with gospel commitment what the Liturgy of the Hours calls us over and over again every day to be.

We must become centers of reflection, centers of conscience, centers of spiritual development, centers of human service, centers of equality, centers of ecumenical interaction, centers of social critique.

Monastic Communities
Must Become Centers of Reflection
on the Faith

The purpose of prayer in the life of a monastic community is not simply to say it; it is to be shaped and formed by it, excited and troubled by it, challenged and confronted by it in those empty spaces in our own lives where the voice of God is yet to be heard. Those for whom prayer is the center of their life must be prepared to enable others to search out its implications for themselves, as well—not as teachers who have all the answers but as disciples who are not afraid of the questions.

Monastic communities that create faith-sharing groups aimed at applying the scriptures to life as we know it today build bridges between the private prayer life of the average in-dividual to the aching hearts of the whole people of God. Like the psalmist, they enable people to hear the cry of the poor.

One of the most common temptations of the spiritual life is to use it to justify our own disinterest in the life of the world around us. Isolated monastics attend peace vigils—but their own communities do not hold them. A few members of the community sign petitions in an attempt to save the rain forests but the community itself has no policy on organic gardening. Individuals read articles on current affairs but they are never used for table reading, never included in community prayer, never become the subject matter of retreat discussions or chapter decisions.

We become communities without a beating heart. And we call ourselves holy for it.

People come to our monasteries to celebrate the liturgy but join other groups to find a way to live a holy life in the middle of the city. They do not look to monasticism to be the spiritual light that enables them to choose between alternatives.

Monastic Communities Must Become
Centers of Conscience

The monastic community that stands for nothing but itself is soon of little value in the lives of others. How is it that we expect other people to live differently, to speak out on issues of the day, to examine the moral implications of legislation that takes from the poor to give to the rich but never do it ourselves?

There was a time when we gave ourselves and everything we had to educate a deprived Catholic population in a society unduly hostile to Catholics. We paid the price for doing it and never considered the action "political"—though hardly a more political action could have been devised in the heydays of anti-Catholicism in this White Anglo-Saxon Protestant country. Now we tell ourselves that a community commitment to support small farmers in the area in which we live, to eliminate racism in our schools, to eliminate sexism from our textbooks and public prayers is somehow or other improper while those made poor of body, poor of spirit by those things languish at the gate.

To talk about the Rule and not to talk about a peace that is broader than ourselves may be, if history is any guide at all, the most unmonastic witness we could possibly give.

To live in the world as if being contemplative gives us the right to ignore the gospel we preach and teach and make the sign of our lives, however well-meaning we are in the process, may well be a distortion of the vocation which, the Vatican documents remind us, is "the prophetic dimension" of the church.

Small wonder, then, that the world looks again at monasticism as having run its course.

In nineteenth-century Germany, monasteries were permitted to reopen as long as they performed some useful service for the society around them. Surely, one of the useful services the world has the right to expect from those whose lives are centered in prayer and contemplation is the fruit of that contemplation.

Who may we expect to expose the effects of social legislation on the poorest of the poor if we do not?

Who will see it as part of their lives to counter the kind of pious moralism that passes for religion with a spirituality that is co-creative, if that kind of thinking never comes out of Benedictine monasteries? Who can we hope will dignify women in their liturgies, their language and their project planning if not communities of Benedictines, for whom discrimination of any kind was foreign to a rule written in the most discriminatory of societies?

Monastic Communities Must Become Centers of Spiritual Development

The days of a flourishing Catholic school system where the smallest towns in the United States of America had a Catholic church or school on all four corners of the main street are long gone. Where will the next generation get its training in spiritual development if not in the monasteries themselves?

Early monastic communities took children into their midst to train them, to educate them, to teach them the essentials of the faith.

Some of those who became oblates of the community stayed there for years. Others linked themselves to the spirituality of the monastic life by public promises and lived and died faithful to the lay Benedictine life.

Perhaps it is time to reinstitute those temporary live-in programs so that men and women of all ages can find in the monasteries of the country what they cannot find in their parishes: full immersion in a spiritual tradition that enables them to see life through the filters of the gospel.

It may be time for us to see ourselves more as spirituality centers for the people of an area than simply degree-granting institutions. Or worse, empty remnants of an era that was once highly productive, but which is now largely long gone.

These kinds of programs have been the mainstay of Buddhism and Hinduism. Monasteries, served by a core community of perpetually professed members, provide at least a year's training for every member of the society. This cadre then becomes both the mainstay of the monastery and the ongoing light of the tradition in the center of the system. They become the lay carriers of both the tradition and the spiritual life. Unless and until Christian monasticism finds some kind of similar integration of monastic values and spirit with the larger society, the light that was once the undying torch of European spirituality can only become dimmer and dimmer by the year. In fact, if we examine the flow of young people in and out of monasteries these days who come for a while and then leave, aren't we simply doing what we fail to institutionalize and, therefore, do better?

Monastic Communities Must Become Centers of Public Service

The Rule that welcomes strangers every hour of the day or night, the tradition that taught Europe to farm and read, the institution that responded to slavery with the practice of entrance-based rank rather than hierarchy is a tradition of service.

Clearly, monastic service is not simply the creation of some sort of product like farm produce or diplomas or hospitality. Monastic service is meant to highlight what is not being done in a society. It is meant to bring the attention of the world to what is not being done by raising it to consciousness itself. When the poor are hungry, it may be soup kitchens. When the excluded are women, it may be inclusion. When the forgotten are the sexually abused, it may be psychological help. When the public disease is violence, it may be programs on anger management.

The point is that it must be more than business-as-usual if society as it is now is to be healed of its sicknesses, exposed in its political nakedness, brought to consciousness about its hidden evils. Good people don't want to spend $150 for sneakers that were made by an Indian child for $.06 an hour. But someone has to organize good people to respond to such things in the name of God or they will never be seen to have moral value. "After all," the corporations rationalize, "they're better off with us than without us, aren't they?"—a loose translation of which must surely be, "They're better off with our injustice than without it, aren't they?"

The cloistered community which—in the name of cloister— does not choose the books in its library carefully to make the connection between personal and public spirituality, that has no posters saying "Nuclear bombs are a sin against humanity" (Pope Paul VI), that never calls attention to the needs of the poor in its mailings, fails the very concept of cloister itself. The purpose of cloister is to focus our attention on the things of God. Since when were the poor, violence, oppression not the things of God? "I have heard the voice of the poor," God says to Moses, "and I am sending you to deliver them."

The message may be as apt for monastic communities to-day as it was for Moses then. Monasticism is not an excuse for inaction. When it is used to create an image of piety acceptable to the powerful, the wealthy, the secure who have the power to make a difference in the lives of the forgotten ones, monasticism has failed. When it cares more for its own acceptable public image than for the concerns of the poor, it has surrendered its prophetic voice to religious niceties and the prophets of the court.

Monasticism Must Be a Model of Interfaith Interaction

With the world on the brink of culture wars masking as religious commitment and wide enough to engulf the entire globe, monastics, of all people, must move into the public arena to extend hands, to show respect, to listen and to learn about the word of God to the other, about the experience of life from the perspective of the other, about the spiritual insights of the other.

Only religion can possibly stop the violence being used in its name. "The world cannot find peace," Kofi Annan said, "without the cooperation of the religions of the world." Monasticism predates the religious ruptures of the West. In its contemplative dimensions, it is the one authentic bond between East and West. It is the link between the spiritual mind of one and the spiritual heart of the other. In monasticism, all the religions understand one another, speak the same language, seek the same God, hear the same message of peace and transcendence, of unity and human wholeness.

Monasticism has a great role to play in the present age—if only we can see beyond our past successes to become again what once we were.

Monasticism Must Be a Model of Equality

The order that traces its origin and growth, its insights and impulse to both St. Scholastica and St. Benedict—to the twin instincts of both women and men—need to claim that joint heritage more clearly, more courageously than ever. We must be to one another what we wish for all the women and men of the world: equally visible, equally respected, equally involved in the articulation and expression of this thing we call "monasticism."

We cannot be bastions of sexism in a world where half the population of the human race has almost nothing to say about their own lives. In monastic communities of this age, special attention must surely be paid to the needs and development of women in faith, in liturgy, in spirituality and in public voice. Benedictine communities must respect and publish the work of both male and female writers. We must include on our altars both men and women. We must make room for the spiritual expression and moral agency of women as well as the theological history of men. We must support in the church those things that assure the full spiritual participation of women, as well as of men.

Without doubt, the world in which we live now needs, as it did in Benedict's time, reflection, conscience, spiritual development, human service, equality, ecumenical interaction and social critique. To be seen as significant enough to attract others to such a life, Benedictines must spend their own lives to make it real.

It may not be so much the discovery of a "new" vision of monasticism we need as a rediscovery of the old one—the one that turned peasants into thinking monastics whose opinions were valued and whose thought was encouraged, the one that gave new dignity to commoners and showed Europe how to rebuild itself, the one that guaranteed that the light of learning would not go out as the world searched again for light.

We have new needs now but the light is no less threatened by them, the dignity of many is still at stake, the ideas of the masses are still being ignored. The financial nobility is back in charge. Where is the new vision monasticism must bring of what it will take to be truly human, truly equal, truly holy now? Where are the new populations on which we are spending our lives?

The fact is that we cannot live in the world as if we were not here, as if tending the Garden were not as much as our responsibility as it is the responsibility of others.

We cannot be centers of authoritarianism in the name of obedience when half the world is demanding to be included in the decision-making processes that involve them. Instead we must begin by developing environments that bring our own members to full adult agency and participation and then including others in our projects, our statements, our concerns, as well, so that we all grow to full stature together.

Fulton Sheen is said to have remarked once, "My concern for religious life is that its members will be fit only for the sandboxes of heaven." Apocryphal statement or not, it is a prescient one. We cannot use religion and contemplation, Benedictinism and obedience as an excuse for not growing up.

We cannot continue to model hierarchical models of dependence and underdevelopment in our members in the name of God's will while whole peoples struggle for the right of self-determination.

We cannot be centers of withdrawal from the questions of the world and purport to be steeped in the word of God, truly contemplative, totally aware of God's will for the world.

We cannot sanctify self-centeredness in the name of a contemplation that hears but sows no seed, bears no fruit, nurtures nothing.

In its dedication to a new vision, monasticism itself will become new again. Structures will change. Ministries will change. Community organization will change. And yet, they will certainly remain emphatically, effectively the same.

Trees are cut down, pruned, in order to cut away the old growth so out of the same roots new life can spring. When we do that, we have the right to assure ourselves that "cut down, it ever grows again." *Succisa virescit,* indeed. But only if we ourselves are willing to prune the old growth so that the new growth can be as strong, as vibrant, as clear as in the past. That's the reality of the thing, not the myth.

23.

The Monastic Spirit and the
Pursuit of Everlasting Beauty

"Tell me about Brother Thomas," the visitor said. "Is he an artist or a monk?"

"He's both," I said.

"But how can that be?" the visitor said. "He's artist-in-residence at your monastery. Do you take men in your community, too?"

"No," I said, "we don't take them. But some of them, like Thomas Bezanson, simply come like moths to the flame of monasticism and never really leave it." And he did.

There is, in fact, history enough to prove the point. Monasticism and art have been forever conjoined, always a marriage of equals. Monasticism without high art has either lost its mission or has not yet become what it sets out to be. Art, without the underlying values upon which monasticism rests, stands to die still-born, not mature enough to be impacting, not perceptive enough to be called art.

No wonder, then, that the bond between monasticism and art goes down so deep and back so far.

Medieval monasteries were centers of the arts and patrons of the arts. Art, as a reflection of beauty, itself an attribute of God, became to be understood, in fact, as simply another expression of incarnation. The presence of God in imaginal forms, Western theologians argued in response to the commonly recurring question, was not heresy. On the contrary. Sacred images, they said, transcended nature. They overcame the distractions of matter. They superseded the merely human. Instead, art gave both linkage and expression to the presence of God in time.

Art, as a result, became an arm of theology and artists the theologians who gave us new ways to see the unseeable. Soaring spires, awesome cloisters and grand chapter houses became the hallmarks of monastic life. Beauty, monastics reasoned, was of the essence of the life. If anything, they had a responsibility to nurture it.

Not surprisingly, then, artistry emerged from the monastic commitment to seek God and artists flocked to the monastery to make visible the infinite dimensions of the invisible God. The artist and the monastic were seeking the same thing. They were embarked on the same journey. They were devoted to the same end. They both believed that spirit was greater than matter but that matter was its borning place.

So, artists lived in the monastery, worked there, produced there all their lives. They did chapel murals and great statuary; they did monastic buildings and Olympian mosaics; they did oil paintings and illuminations and brilliant ceramics and textiles. Monasteries and monastic churches drew artists like magnets attracted iron.

Artists both belonged to the monastery and did not belong, at least in the institutional sense. Some were vowed monastics whose lives were given to the illumination of manuscripts and the creation of sacred objects, the sculpting of liturgical ornaments, and the design of grand tapestries and holy vestments. Others were artists or lay monks who spent their lives drawing plans and doing the stonework and glass that became over time the great monasteries and monastic churches of Europe to which they had attached themselves.

Whatever their canonical definitions, lay or ordained, professed monastics or lay oblates, they embodied the symbiotic relationship that existed between the two—between the essence of monasticism and the essence of art—and which the two took for granted but seldom bothered to articulate.

At the same time, the culture knew that somehow monasteries spawned artists and that monastics themselves were the most pointed expression of the human dimension of sacred art.

Brother Thomas is a living example of both realities.

Brother Thomas Bezanson moved out of one monastery, he said, so he could dedicate his life to pottery and then moved into another one for the same reason.

One way or another, Thomas has been in a monastery for over fifty years, most of his adult life, all of his professional life. Strange, some would think now, in this day and age. After all, isn't an artist an artist, a monastic a monastic? What can possibly be the linkage between the two? But Thomas likes to say that for a number of those years he was a monastic who was also a potter. Then he discovered that he was a potter who was also a monastic.

The distinction bears thinking about. It tells us something about both monasticism and art. Monasticism exists in pursuit of the beauty of the invisible God. Art makes shining slivers of that beauty visible. To develop the soul, then, is to develop the essence of an artist.

Monasticism, in a special way, does not simply value the link between spirit and art, it creates it. "Beauty," Michelangelo wrote, "is the purgation of superfluities." Monasticism is the one path of life that declares itself to be the single-minded search for God in life, before which all other pursuits pale. It sets out to excise whatever exists to obscure the awareness of what the contemplative calls the "one thing necessary."

Monasticism is the most piercing expression of the search for truth, the conscious investigation of the marrow of what it means to be fully human. The monastic gives life over to the search for the spirit in life that makes matter holy and the spiritual attainable. Monasticism is about more than living every day well. It is an exercise in living every day on a plane above itself, of seeing in the obvious more than the obvious, in finding even in the mundane the creative energy that drives creation to heights beyond itself. If, indeed, truth is beauty and beauty truth, then the monastic and the artist are one.

Monasticism, in fact, cultivates the artistic spirit. Basic to monasticism are the very qualities art demands of the artist: silence, contemplation, discernment of spirits, community and humility. Basic to art are the very qualities demanded of the monastic: single-mindedness, beauty, immersion, praise and creativity.

The merger of one with the other makes for great art; the meaning of one for the other makes for great soul.

It is in silence that the artist hears the call to raise to the heights of human consciousness those qualities no definitions can ever capture. Ecstasy, pain, fluid truth pass us by so quickly or surround us so constantly that the eyes fail to see and the heart ceases to respond. It is in the awful grip of ineffable form or radiant color that we see into a world that is infinitely beyond our natural grasp, yet only just beyond our artist's soul.

It is contemplation that leads an artist to preserve for us forever the essence of a thing that takes us far beyond its accidents. Only by seeing the unseen within can the artist dredge it out of nothingness so that we can touch it, too.

It is a capacity for the discernment of spirits that enables an artist to recognize real beauty from plastic pretensions to it, from cheap copies of even cheaper attempts at it. The artist distills for the world to see the one idea, the fresh form, the stunning grandeur of moments which the world has begun to take for granted or has failed even to notice, or, worse, has now reduced to the mundane.

It is a love for human community that puts the eye of the artist in the service of truth. Knowing the spiritual squalor to which the pursuit of less than beauty can lead us, the artist lives to stretch our senses beyond the tendency to settle for lesser things—sleazy stories instead of great literature, superficial caricatures of bland characters rather than great portraits of great souls, flowerpots instead of pottery.

Finally, it is humility that enables an artist to risk rejection and failure, disdain and derogation to bring to the heart of the world what the world too easily, too randomly—too callously—overlooks.

Charles Péguy wrote: "We must always tell what we see. Above all, and this is more difficult, we must always see what we see." Brother Thomas is a truth-teller in the great tradition of all those artists who spend their lives straining to see the Truth and then trying to help the rest of us see it, as well.

Brother Thomas is an artist formed in the monastic art of the pursuit of Beauty. He is single-minded, in awe of the beauty that makes life, life, immersed in the center of it, in praise of the power of it, in search of the creativity that captures it for us now, again, forever, always.

Amen. Alleluia for such a one as this.

Thomas has been brother, standard-bearer of beauty, pursuer of the spiritual and holder of the heart of holiness of which monasticism speaks and which it pursues in time and out of time, in the sacred—and in the profane.

Clearly, great art is a very spiritual thing. More, a great spiritual life is itself a piece of great art. It is the ultimate creativity. To Thomas God said, "Let there be art," and, behold, it came to be.

24.

Monasticism in a Mobile World

After more than fifty years of life in a monastery, I have begun to sift and sort the effects of it all, asking myself, what—if
anything—of monastic life is worth passing on to others in
this day and age? What of this life has any impact or import to
populations other than monastic communities themselves—and
how can those outside traditional monasteries, too, join throngs
of monastics over the centuries who have found this life both
enriching and enlightening?

Monasticism is the one spiritual discipline that is at the heart
of every major tradition and crosses every religious boundary—
Hinduism, Buddhism, Islam and Judaism. Every age, every path,
has answered the questions of the spiritual dimensions of life in
ways peculiar to itself, in language and symbols and lifestyles it
could understand. For some, in the past, the search to unite with
the One, with the Energy, with the Life of life, took the form of
desert asceticism. For others, it lay in community and communal worship. For many, it was an attempt to withdraw from the
business of this world in order to be better attuned to the next.

But for Benedict of Nursia, a young lay man in sixth-century
Rome, the spiritual life lay in simply living this life, our daily
life, well. All of it. Every simple, single action of it. History attests

to the power of such a life lived to turn the ordinary into an experience of the extraordinary union with the God of the Universe—here and now. Benedictine spirituality, the legacy of this sixth-century founder of cenobitic monasticism in the West, is to our own times proof of its enduring value.

Spirituality based on the Rule of Benedict, a communal lifestyle, is over fifteen hundred years old. It developed at a time when Europe lay in political, economic, communal and social disarray. And it exists around the world to this day. Anything that survives the ages with new vitality in every age is surely worthy of serious spiritual examination in our own.

The fact is that the sixth-century Rule of Benedict has shown a plasticity, a penchant for both adjustment to new conditions as well as meaningful adaptation of its basic values and practices common to few institutions anywhere. Most significant, perhaps, is that instead of setting out to reform the decadence around him, Benedict of Nursia transcended the social system of the time and offered the world a new and fresh way of living dailiness with great spiritual depth. He ignored the cheap and chaotic superficiality of sixth-century Rome and, instead, gathered others around him to live according to different standards, to walk a different path, to live the life everyone else lived—but differently. Through the ages, thousands of others have done the same. As a result, Benedictine monasticism has evolved from age to age, until many different forms of its past impulses exist yet—but all of them as carriers of the original impulse.

Today, in this time of cataclysmic social upheavals, of global transitions, of technological breakthroughs of unimagined proportions and uncertain effects, we must do the same. Old patterns are breaking down; individuals, families and small groups everywhere—in intentional communities and home worship, in parishes and prayer groups, through committed lifestyles and private disciplines—are seeking to shape new ways of living for themselves in the shell of the old.

Ironically, it is this oldest spiritual tradition in the Western world that gives us the greatest hope of success. The major question about Benedictine spirituality is not how did it manage to stay the same through so many reeling centuries. The answer to Benedictine longevity lies not in its changelessness but in its ability to change consistently, century after century, without loss or damage to the heart and soul of it. The ability to relate to every generation, to speak to every spiritual need, to live both in the present, mobile world but not of it, is the strength of Benedictine spirituality and model of life it presents to the world age after age.

Monasteries today—once almost exclusively large academic centers or local parish programs—must now describe for themselves wider arcs of influence and insight. They must become centers of contemplation, centers of conscience, centers of social service, and centers of monastic spiritual development that people can seek and find on their computers, the new instrument of connection and influence in this time. The needs are urgent now.

Centers of Contemplation

The purpose of prayer in the life of a monastic community is not simply to say it; it is to be shaped and formed by it. Those for whom prayer is the center of their life must be prepared to enable others to search out its implications for themselves, as well—not as teachers who have all the answers but as disciples who are not afraid of the questions.

Lectio Divina, the Benedictine bridge to a contemplative lifestyle, belongs in every Benedictine bulletin, on every website, in every program on prayer. How else can we lead as well as talk?

Centers of Conscience

Monastic service is meant to highlight what is not being done in a society. It is meant to bring the attention of the world to what is missing in the world by raising it to consciousness itself. When the poor are hungry, it may be by the opening of monastery soup kitchens. When the excluded are women, it may be their inclusion in the choir that best signals a world of equals. When the forgotten are the sexually abused, it may be emotional support and understanding that heals the wounds. When the public disease is violence, it may be programs on nonviolent protest and public reconciliation that are most needed. The point is that we must somehow point to the distance between the world we live in and the gospel we preach.

Centers of Social Service

Where there are Benedictines, the gospel must be spoken plainly, like Jesus on the road from Galilee to Jerusalem and Benedict with the Goth. In a world based on class and power it is our place to help people see in the gospel the impetus, the call, for social change. Led by the monasteries with whom they associate, lay people can find a way into the needs and the pain, the power and the hope of society around them. They can become active members of community-led justice projects and social advocacy programs.

Centers of Monastic Spiritual Development

Over 15 percent of the population of the globe now say that they claim no religion at all. In the United States, it's 21 percent. Of those under thirty-four, it's 33 percent.

In the United States, too, "Nones" are the second largest "denomination" in the country. All of these people have left somebody's church, parish, congregation, because they say they found nothing there spiritual enough to keep them.

This age must also realize that "spiritual but not religious" has become a major marker of religious identity. These people are seekers who say that the institution itself is a block to their being able to find the spiritual sustenance they seek.

It is for those reasons that Mount St. Benedict Monastery, in Erie, Pennsylvania, USA, has developed a new community outreach program to provide Benedictine spirituality for all seekers of a monastic bent. Its name, "Monasteriesoftheheart. org," signals its basic structure: a web-based Benedictine community for seekers who stand in the midst of a shimmering world of options—spiritual as well as secular. Most of these options are clearly rich in resources but lack at base the tradition needed to give both substance and certainty to the seeker. Overwhelmed by choices, modern seekers look longingly for the rhythm of a better life, a model upon which to build their own lives, a template to take through the maze of empty promises, seductive dead ends and useless panaceas that a spiritless world has to offer.

The difference in the role and place of monasteries founded centuries before us and the quandaries faced by our own in this new age lies in the revolution of lifestyles from the agrarian to the digital age. For centuries people found us. Local monasteries offered a spiritual home, often work, always hospitality, forever a depth of prayer and contemplation in the monasteries of the area. People flocked to the monasteries for the physical support, spiritual depth and personal guidance the monasteries provided. Now, in societies far-flung, mobile, more characterized by population differences than sameness, it is our turn to find them, to ring the monastery bells in other places and in new ways.

As a result, part and parcel of every institution in this new era is the question, "Where are the people?" The answer is at once frustrating and enticing. The answer is, "The people—the young, the professional, the old, the isolated, the lonely, the seekers—are all on-line, on the internet, on their computers, in their search programs." And that's where we need to be, as well.

What Benedict did was simple, but revolutionary.

First, he began a new lay tradition. Second, he seeded small communities that offered an alternative to the culture of the time. Monasteries of the Heart attempts to do the same thing for this age—but differently. It is a new kind of web-based community that provides *Lectio Divina,* community prayer, learning and spirituality programs for a world that is also new.

Monasteries of the Heart—following the ancient Rule of Benedict still constant in Benedictine monasteries everywhere—is meant to be a new way to live a monastic life in the center of the world today. It is not meant to abandon traditional Benedictinism in favor of some new or exotic spiritual practice. On the contrary, it is centered in the Rule, rooted in its values. It is, instead, an apple falling off an ancient tree, a cutting meant to grow steeped in its history, fresh in its form. Individuals, families, small intentional communities—those alone, embedded in groups and captives of groups for physical, medical or social reasons they did not choose—who seek to create within themselves a Monastery of the Heart can also find there the God who is forever seeking us.

Since its founding in 2011, over seventeen thousand people have become members of Monasteries of the Heart. More than thirteen hundred members have participated in one or more of the twenty courses and retreats offered on the website. More than ten thousand visit the prayer page that changes weekly on a regular basis. Over five thousand have participated in the exercises of *Lectio Divina,* more than two thousand have joined with other members in performing the suggested "Good Works" and ten Monasteries of the Heart communities are meeting in prisons as over thirty-five of the on-line and onsite communities embedded in Monasteries of the Heart also do in their own homes. Monasteries of the Heart gives an anchor, a ladder and a path to all that. It immerses members in the contemplation of the God-life within and fosters a contemplative view of the world itself.

In all that data, in all those realizations, it becomes clear again why this new kind of Benedictine community exists and why web-based programs and other experimental and creative programs offered and guided by the monasteries themselves need to be launched just as, at one time, we risked founding small monasteries in the hinterlands of the world.

Monasticism offers a spiritual journey grounded in a way of life that is ever ancient, ever new. Benedictine monasticism has outlived every century for the last fifteen hundred years. Clearly, monasticism has something to say to the here and now wherever and whenever that here and now may be.

Monasticism teaches the presence of God in life. It engages the human soul in a consciousness of God that illuminates every dark moment of life and confirms the love of God however commonplace the present.

Monasticism does not require spiritual heroics; it requires spiritual consciousness of the power of simplicity, humility, equality and care of the earth.

Monasticism brings us to understand the sanctifying dimension of human community. It leads us to care for one another as God has cared for us.

Monasticism is here, too, to encourage lay people to fashion for themselves—either alone or in groups—contemplative monasteries of justice and peace, equality and universal heart. Wherever they are. So that others can find in Benedictinism once again the wisdom and strength of the ages.

In its dedication to a new vision, monasticism itself will become new again. Structures will change. Ministries will change. Community organization will change. And yet, they will certainly remain emphatically, effectively the same.

Trees are cut down, pruned, in order to cut away the old growth so out of the same roots new life can spring. When we do that, we have the right to assure ourselves that "cut down, it ever grows again." *Succisa virescit,* is the Benedictine motto and myth. But only if we ourselves are willing to prune the old growth so that the new growth can be as strong, as vibrant, as clear as the past. That's the reality of the thing, not the myth.

25.

Being Benedictine

"To be or not to be:
that is the question"

Six ancient stories frame what "being Benedictine" is really all about. First, to simply "be" Benedictine is to be registered on the institution's roles, to be a card-carrying member of one of the most long-standing spiritual institutions in the church.

It is to own over fifteen hundred years of history and to carry it like a spiritual passport in a copy of the old, small, simple Rule of Benedict with its twenty chapters of spiritual counsels and fifty small chapters of proscriptions.

In fact, the Rule does not proscribe much in detail at all. It stresses only that all the details of life need to be attended to—frankly, as any group does. That's what it means to "be Benedictine," to be a well-organized, predictable lifestyle.

But *being* Benedictine—being—in heart and soul—now that is something different.

Being Benedictine requires us to mean something real today—to shine a light into today's darkness, to live as Jesus lived—with integrity and courage not in a particular century, but in every century.

That's something that develops from era to era, bearing its values with it as it moves across time but shaping them to fit the age it's in. And that makes all the difference between to be a Benedictine and being a Benedictine.

First of all, it is the struggle to avoid becoming fossilized ourselves—by allowing pious routines to substitute for being spiritually genuine and dynamic.

Being Benedictine is not a list of rules; that would be easy! It is about spending a lifetime immersed in contemplation living for human community and displaying a quality of heart that beats for something bigger than ourselves.

In fact, being Benedictine is so much more impacting on the society around us than simply keeping a check list of spiritual tasks. But if that's the case, then the question is, Where do we go to see this in action, in order to become it ourselves?

The fact is that a very ancient book has preserved it for us. Among the things Pope Gregory the Great, sixth-century ruler, reformer and writer, left behind to influence the church for centuries was his hagiography of powerful Italian saints.

Entitled the *Dialogues,* the most famous of its four volumes, is his metaphorical presentation of Benedict of Nursia, the founder of cenobitic monasticism.

The book is not historical—meaning it is not a biographical recitation of Benedict's life: his birth, family, education, or a chronicle of his professional leadership. No, Gregory's book is a poetic description—a common literary genre of the period—of the soul of the man Benedict. It presents us with symbolic instances of Benedict's values, spiritual strength and moral integrity in action.

But even there something very unusual happens. Gregory, in the *Dialogues,* does not talk about the content, the length or even the mystical dimension of Benedict's prayer life. Gregory talks only about the effects, only the effects, of Benedict's prayer life on others.

Benedict's strength of soul, his spiritual impact on others is, for Gregory, the real marrow of Benedictine life, not the mechanics or rituals of his prayer schedule or of ours.

So, I want to talk—as Gregory does—about what Benedictine life really meant then and so today.

First, the Rule is clear. Benedictine prayer has three layers of soulfulness: choral prayer, spiritual reading and lectio. The constant repetition of the call to prayer, the scheduled times for reading, the demands of lectio mark the beat of every monastic day.

They draw us back again and again to the nucleus of the life; they refuse to allow us to drift away from the call within us, as in Jesus, to grow in wisdom, to age with depth, and to shine, as Jesus did, with the courage of the Spirit. They remind us that contemplation is the rudder of the monastic heart.

As a result, the real Benedictine is always in touch with the will of God for the world. Rooted in the timelessness of the psalms and scriptures, we absorb the story of God's ways with the world, as a model for our own responses to life now.

No, Benedictine spirituality is not about the past. It is always about the presence of God in time—this time, our time, my time and yours.

And Gregory tells us a story that demonstrates the truth of Benedict's concern for the complexities of now: It tells us that when Benedict abandoned his studies to go into solitude, the nurse who had cared for him since childhood stayed with him still.

One day, she borrowed a tray to clean the wheat but the tray fell—and broke in two. With no way to repair it and no money to replace it, the nurse burst into tears. Benedict saw the pain, picked up the pieces, knelt over them, and cried to God for help. Then, Gregory says, the two pieces joined together again—the tray was whole; no relationships were ruptured, his love and care for her had been a healing gift.

What can we learn here about being Benedictine? We learn that being Benedictine means that we, too, must weep with those who weep. We learn that the lives of the little ones of the world depend on us.

Clearly, to pray well is to love well, to include within our own hearts, the heartbreak of others.

What the world needs now are witnesses of care for the planet and its peoples, for a world that lives on "the will of God first," not "America first." It is the consciousness of God's will that makes Benedictine prayer life a communal gift.

Prayer is meant to fix the eye of the soul on the real purpose of life when the common challenges of life seem mundane.

Most of all, we see that it is not the sum of the prayers we pray that counts. It's simply not about length. It is the way our prayer life challenges our own hearts and lives daily—the way it makes us more centered in God, and more aware of our own limitations—and, at the same time, it's the way it directs our own role in the God-life around us that determines its quality.

It fixes us on the life of Jesus who went from place to place doing good. As must we touch the poor, challenge the national budget, speak for oppressed women and contest the rising control of human wealth by a few in the face of the many deprived of the essentials of life as we sit here.

No doubt about it: Benedictine contemplation is deeper than a prayer schedule. It is meant to make us truly contemplative, people who see all of life through the eyes and the heart of God.

But more than for choral prayer Benedict calls, secondly, for a great deal of study in the Rule.

The practice of continuing to educate ourselves in sacred subjects, on important topics, like the tension between Galileo and the Church, for instance, is meant to increase our insights into the parts of life that need new witness, new understanding even now, maybe.

Or, more likely, perhaps, we must study to understand the human need for ecological sustainability and our moral responsibilities as Christians to care for the earth in a time of technological exploitation.

These subjects recall us to the glory of Creation and make us capable of speaking in its name until, finally, in the third place, we come to realize the power of lectio.

Lectio is more than spiritual reading, more than a commitment to our spiritual education. Lectio is about our personal engagement with the word of God. It's about the stretching of us, the shaping within us, of what it takes to have a monastic heart. Lectio leads us to wrestle with meaning, with mystery, with the mettle of the Word of God in a soul-to-soul infusion into our spiritual bloodstream as God and I go through life together.

Lectio is the conversation we open with God—sometimes about the importance of a single word, like faith, maybe; sometimes with a whole idea of witness, maybe; until, after days, maybe even months, of struggle with such demanding ideas— we feel God's searing, revealing call to face the changes we will need to make to become what the Word is calling us to do as we begin to realize what being Benedictine demands.

Prayer leads us to follow the Jesus we seek. Spiritual reading enables us to let the message of Jesus into our lives and lectio begins the struggle to understand what the Word calls us to at this moment and being it begins to mean more than simply thinking about it. It has changed us.

We become pliable now, less afraid of change, open-hearted and ready for the future, more mature spiritually, even more stable psychologically. What we have learned by now about being Benedictine now lives in us.

We are ready now in heart and spirit, to right the broken trays of life, to give ourselves to the pain and struggle of others because we know "God with us"; God as always within us. And we are able to keep going on being Benedictine in the world.

But there is another dimension of being Benedictine today that is beyond the simple patterns of medieval cenobitic life: Secondly, community and relationships are of its essence. There is in Benedictinism a quality that is its hidden core. The pictures of monastics wrapped up inside layers of protective wool, eyes down, hands clasped over the self can be read as a sign of social separation or rigid individualism, or, at very least, in our time, a kind of lostness in God alone.

And sure enough, God alone is the romantic explanation of being Benedictine. But God in us is the sanctifying impulsion that requires us to exist for others as much as for ourselves, to live community as much as we do our individuality.

It is God in us that calls us to be God's presence, God's care for others, God's support, in the here and now. God in us calls us to extend ourselves for others as God has for us. It is God in us—our community with God—that is the basis of human community. By seeing everyone else as co-creators of God's world, as well as ourselves, the world becomes our common home and all its peoples our community.

Written in a period of social collapse, of colonial oppression, of ethnic divides, of slavery and classism and patriarchal privilege, on the brink of what historians call AD 536, the worst year ever in the western world, the Rule of Benedict becomes then a model of justice, a beacon of equality, a sign of peace between strangers which we, now, must rekindle in every age.

Relationships, Benedict teaches in Chapter 7, "On Humility," are the crux of our own human and spiritual development.

It is our relationship with God, our relationship with our guides and mentors, our honesty about ourselves and the quality of our relationship with others that is the measure of our own psychological growth as well as our spiritual adulthood. It is the bonding of differences that made Benedictinism a social force as

Benedictines organized a new social system in a shattered society where communities were not based on rank, on social status, on age, on wealth, on education, or on gender in a world fractured by violence, inequality and exploitation.

Historians say to this day that it was Benedictinism—this wild weave of scattered relationships into one civil union—that saved Western civilization after the Fall of Rome.

But community is not a geography. It is a matter of heart and mind. It cannot be created by place alone and it cannot be destroyed by distance alone. It is of the essence of the soul.

In a period of massive immigration, seeping borders, abandoned children, homeless families, unemployed men and women, new racism, blatant sexism, fear aplenty of the other, and more wealth in an impoverished world than the world has ever seen, being Benedictine may be the most impacting presence we could ever be.

When you speak for these poor, demonstrate for these outcasts, serve these simple ones, you become a wall against the total breakdown of humanity on this planet at this time.

Community simply means that we're in this together. All of us: the poor, the powerful, the underlings, because we are speaking for them. Shining a lamp into their darkness. Refusing to ignore the wants of the world in the light of our own security we are now "a voice crying in the wilderness," ceaselessly.

When everyone else wants to block out the awkward, pleading, embarrassing beggary—arms outstretched, hands open—being Benedictine means that we must be community builders. But community building does not just happen. It cannot be taken for granted.

Gregory describes the extent of Benedict's community building this way: When Benedict was in his room, one of the monks, the boy Placid, went to the lake to get water, lost his balance, slipped—and the current was carrying him away.

When Benedict saw the situation, he cried out, "Brother Maurus, Hurry! Hurry, Brother Maurus, Hurry." And Maurus, driven by the urgency of the call, ran with all his might over the very top of the water, grabbed Placid by the hair of his head and dragged him to shore. And Maurus said of it, "I did not even know that I did it."

The learning is fundamental: Everyone needs a wisdom figure—as Benedict was for Maurus.

Wisdom figures model faith, spiritual commitment and the trust that spurs us on—even in darkness—to realize that care for human community is always a call to me. Then when others around us are drowning and help is in scarce supply, it will be the call of community around us that will bring us all together again back to shore. In fact, what being Benedictine needs now in order to respond well is a very new definition of community.

Yes, the kind of community for which the ancient Rule of Benedict is written, is based on a great deal of physical presence in a given physical area. But as the world enlarges, so does the concept of community itself. The physical is still important, yes, but not only and differently. Now community is often virtual, but just as real in many dimensions as sitting next to the same person in chapel our entire lives.

Being Benedictine means that what is important is that together we each be an extension of the gospel, an extension of each other, and an extension of Benedictine spirituality whether we are together or alone.

What is imperative is that the sharing of the common mind be just as important as once was the sharing of a common schedule, or a common place, or a common work, so that the spirit of community that is being Benedictine to its core may save us each by the other and spread like a holy plague throughout the world.

In this age, whole cultures of people—in one big city after another—all look as if they live together but actually they all live together alone. Being Benedictine is not about looking like a community; it is about being one. In fact, the unsung hero of community building is stability.

Third, stability and listening/obedience become the cement of community. Stability, at one level, is the commitment to grow into the soul of the self by learning from what we are learning around us. Stability, is the Benedictine vow of the commitment to endure, to persist and to develop to the day we die—not despite the burdens of the day but because of them and through them.

Stability is what requires us to grow where we are, where people know us—and because people know us and call us to the more of ourselves. Their insights, their goals and their habits grate and grind against our own until we are both—them and us—more tempered, more understanding, more loving people.

Stability in community, a lifetime of togetherness, brings us to the truth of ourselves—no hiding, no dissembling allowed. Stability is the very grist of our sanctity, the very substance of our promise to care for one another, to bear one another's burdens, to allow ourselves to be known and to grow, to change and be stretched to the wholeness of ourselves as a result of it.

It is through stability—the commitment of monastics not to run away from themselves, not to deny their own limitations, but to realize that what irritates them is exactly what will grow them up to the full stature of themselves—that we learn about ourselves from all the others around us, which will eventually dissolve our pride and bring us to peace, with one another, with life.

Stability is the foundation of obedience—the key to which is learning to listen to what the Spirit is saying to us through the rest of the community. And so it is in regard to stability and obedience that Gregory does the most interesting thing of all— he doesn't tell us about what Benedict did to grow up all the others. Instead, he tells us what happened to Benedict's growth and wisdom thanks to stability and obedience.

Gregory recounts the story of Abbot Benedict and his sister Scholastica who—once a year, Gregory says—came together "to talk about holy things." This time, Scholastica begs him to stay the night to finish the conversation. And he scolds her for even thinking of such a thing. After all, he says, he has to get back to the monastery before dark! It's the Rule!

So she puts her head down on the table and starts to pray, and all of a sudden a vicious storm begins. Realizing that they can't possibly go now, Benedict says, "God forgive you, sister, what have you done?" And Scholastica answered him: in nice, straight, woman-talk. "I asked you for a favor, but you would not listen to me. So I turned to my God and God heard my prayer. So, now leave—if you can."

Learnings: Clearly being Benedictine tells us that the law is never greater than love. And it also tells us that a woman has as much power in the eyes of God as any man and that we, too, must recognize women as our spiritual guides.

Ah, it is ever thus. Think of it: the patriarchal world wants obedience: Military obedience. Blind obedience. Unthinking obedience. It is a hierarchical structure that depends for its success—as well as leads to its failure—by demanding unthinking submission to the values and authorities of the time: power, classism, individualism, nationalism, sexism, racism and sublime servility to the system.

The concept of obedience in a patriarchal world is a far cry from the presentation of obedience in the Rule of Benedict.

Benedict calls us to open our hearts, to think carefully, to consider. Doing so demands that we listen intently to the motives that drive us. Most of all, it is a call to listen to life, to everyone around us and to everything that circumstance has to teach us.

It teaches us to listen, indeed.

> Listen to the tradition.
> Listen to the word of God in scripture.

> Listen to the insights we hear from others.
> Listen to the circumstance and needs of the
>   moment.

It is a call for universal awareness of God at work in every situation of our lives.

Benedict learned all of that from the woman Scholastica. And so we learn, again, that each of us needs to find someone—a soul-friend—who tells us our truth, who encourages our growth and brings light to life along the way.

"Listen," the Rule says, and Scholastica says, "Don't leave now."

Great prayer, deep listening, worthwhile works are the pillars of the monastic life, yes, but they are not its surest metric.

To the ancients—Aristotle, the desert monastics—and in a sense to modern science—the heart was the organ closest to the soul, the seat of human intelligence, the center of all emotions. It was the quality of the monastic heart that determined our personal merit. As Ambo Pando taught disciples: "If you have a heart, you can be saved."

The message from each is clear: Rationality alone is a puny guide; the brain is an insufficient instrument to which to trust our souls. Ideas are not enough to save us. Only ideas filtered through the feelings of life can possibly bring us to an optimal conclusion about life and how to live it.

When the heart goes sour, the human being goes astray, humanity withers and the salvation of our small, hurting world will need to wait for someone else with heart. No amount of rigid religions can save us. Only heart can do that. And that is what Scholastica's miracle of stability taught Benedict.

Monastics are contemplatives but they do not go through life starry-eyed drifters. Work, in fact, is a monastic charism. "We earn our bread by the sweat of our brow," the Rule teaches us, "as did our ancestors before us." So what is it?

Fourth: work and stewardship are what enable us to construct the future. The monastic heart is consciously shaped: it is nurtured by prayer, devoted to the development of human community, stable in its promises and committed to personal growth and, therefore, the monastic works with a purpose and stewards the world with care.

In fact, the work of monastics has four goals: to promote the coming of the Reign of God; to develop the best in the worker as well as in the work; to meet the needs of the world around us; and to steward creation on every level. The monastic heart knows that work is our contribution to the world.

Work is every bit as much a defined part of Benedictine life as are times of prayer and holy reading. It is the daily manual labor, the work of our hands, the kind of work that makes the world a better place for everyone that the Rule requires.

There is no room in the Rule for classism, or racism, or sexism—no room for those who think that what they do are the important things in life. It is actually physical work that demonstrates equality and community, service and mutual support best.

It reminds us that running the vacuum, washing the clothes, doing the dishes, making the beds, bathing the children is what keeps us all—both men and women—aware of the struggles that come with simply getting from day to day.

It is, in fact, these very things that keep us in touch with one another, with those we love and so must also serve.

In the end, work gives us a sense of what it means to be a full human being. Rather than a foreigner in our own homes, or an outlander in our own society, we discover that we are the bearers of the human race. Good work is our contribution to the development of humankind and the fulfillment of the globe. The simple truth is that sloth is not a Benedictine virtue.

And finally, work is our gift to the future, our legacy, our gift of co-creation.

Gregory's story of Benedict's attitude to work and stewardship turns prudence and security upside down. He tells us:

In the famine, the deacon Agapitus came to beg oil from the monastery—for heat, light and food preparation.

Benedict immediately ordered the cellarer to give Agapitus the little oil that the monastery itself had left. But the cellarer, a prudent man, could not bring himself to do it. After all, the monastery needed it.

When Benedict discovered that his order had been ignored, he was angry. He ordered another monk to take the oil jar and throw it out the window. But though the glass jar fell on rock, it did not break. So, Benedict gathered the entire community, rebuked the cellarer in public and in the sight of all told another monk to give the oil away.

Point made.

The learning here simply dashes every capitalist value modern society embraces. It says that there are values beyond security and good sense and it also says that everything we have belongs to the poor.

For the Benedictine, the question of work and stewardship is the moral matter of what it means to be human on a planet we did not create but can destroy.

Being Benedictine means committing ourselves to stand as a sign to the world that whatever work we do must be done with full heart and extra effort, not for our sake alone but for the sake of the development and stewardship of the entire world.

Being Benedictine requires us to realize that the globe is also our responsibility. It is not a civic exercise that being Benedictine is about; it is about the salvation of the world.

Finally, one thing and one thing only—hospitality—undergirds every dimension of Benedictine life. The one who is not like us is to be treated like us at all times in all situations: as Christ.

Finally, hospitality and wisdom. Being Benedictine requires our own reckless communal hospitality to build up the human community among us—in our own monasteries.

Not to talk about it but to do it. To care for the stranger, rather than simply take care of ourselves. It is a weighty matter. It calls on us to support the stranger—to talk to them, to listen to them, to see to their comfort and their needs—to pray among us, to eat with us, to come and go, and do all the little things that are never, ever done: like talking out loud at prayer or walking mud in on the lobby floor, while we listen and listen and listen, even when we're tired, it's late, and we simply want to be alone.

The point is that monastic hospitality is more than carefully catering to, and connecting with, "our kind of people." It is about providing space where all and everyone are welcome, are made at home. From wherever they've come to wherever they're going.

The Rule is specific about the place of strangers in the life of the Benedictine: they are welcome—day and night. "Let an old monastic," the Rule details, "one who cannot roam around—be put at the door so that when anyone comes, the porter may say, '*Benedicite.*'" Bless you for coming and stretching our perfect life. Indeed, bless you for keeping us in touch with reality, with life, with the will of God in the here and now.

The truth is that hospitality is the Benedictine bridge to a world of strangers. Gregory describes the moment in Benedict's life when he makes the outsider an insider:

A wandering farmer, looking for both help and home, attached himself to the monastery and was given the job raking the bank of the lake for safety sake. All of a sudden the farmer flung the rake into the air so hard its cutting head fell far out in deep, deep water. The farmer, aghast and sure of reproof, ran wailing for help.

But however much his regret, it was all for nothing. A piece of important monastery equipment was suddenly lost. And with it, the farmer was sure, his reputation and any hope he'd held for a future there.

When Benedict realized the farmer's plight, he ran to the water's edge, thrust the rake handle into the water and watched the blade rise through the waves to reunite with the stick. Then Benedict said to the farmer, "Don't work so hard; don't worry about it; just go on with your work."

The learnings from all of this? Simple.

Real hospitality comes always from the heart, remember: If you have a heart, you can be saved.

So we are as blessed by those who come to the door in need of a listening heart as they are by us who take them in.

To take strangers in is to give them new life. That farmer and thousands like him attest that people remember how they were received: the immigrants on the border will remember how they were received; the neighbor who just happens to wander in will remember how they were received; the lonely, the empty-hearted, the wanderer without a clear direction, in search of a path to the future, will remember how they were received.

Those who find in us a home for a day, a listener for an hour, a seeker for a lifetime will remember how they were received by those who have a heart or not.

It can be a shock to be told that doing what other people need—what the world needs—is more important spiritually than making for ourselves a spiritual life with a perfect little schedule, and a perfect little prayer life, of perfect privacy and perfect silence so that we can sink into oblivion with closed eyes thinking thoughts of spiritual perfection and grateful to be a Benedictine, but totally unaware that being Benedictine means to share our lives with everyone—and making Benedict's own miracles ours to continue.

The mystic, Benedict, the *Dialogues* tell us, worked miracles: about love that binds the broken trays of the world:

about the common care that is community
building;

about listening to others in order to go on
growing;

about doing good works so that others may
live;

about being spiritual centers—night and day—
to sooth the heavy hearts of some, support
the dreams of others,

Finally, the miracle of the mystic Benedict who looked up into the night sky, saw the darkness fall away and, Gregory teaches us, "saw the whole world in a single ray of light," then passed it on to us in a prejudiced world to make the miracle of hospitality the newer, greater gift of globalism, in our own time and our own hearts.

"The purpose of life is to see," the Zen master tells us, and "The only task worthy of our efforts is to construct the future," Chardin said. If globalism lies at the heart of Benedictine hospitality, in your hands and mine lies fifteen hundred years of a lifestyle which at this great moment confronts us with the major questions of our time: Is to be Benedictine enough for us here in this place and now at this time? Or are we, in this era, intent on being Benedictine enough to launch this tradition into the process of saving Western civilization for another fifteen hundred years?

These questions are of the essence of Benedictinism: the answers are totally ours.

Afterword

Joan Chittister

Sing a new song whatever the cost, so that we all might wake up.

Human development is a slow process that happens in stages of more or less regularity. We call them infancy, early childhood, pre-teen, adolescence, adulthood. As we move through one at a time, each of them a task from birth to death, we keep an eye on the charts that tell us what to expect in each.

Spiritual development, on the other hand, is slower than that. And not guaranteed.

Spiritual development depends on the way we deal with one phase of life after another—with whether we deal with them or not, in fact. There are no rule books to describe the process for us, no time charts, no defined hurdles to conquer—just one small internal mountain after another to reckon with.

The soul is tested from one challenge to another, from one experience to another, from one wisdom figure to another. Literature is full of figures who meet the obstacles of every stage and prevail. Or not. In the end, we begin to understand, our "lives" become what we ourselves fashion out of both those wins and those losses. Of which there are many.

My own development attests to them all. The death of a young father, the struggles of a young mother, the continuous

225

reshaping of a family, the shock and isolation of personal physical limitations, the discovery of the internal self—and the need to come to terms with its wrenched character—the tenor of effects of life in a monastery, the meaning of "belief." Each of those chapters of life draws the contours of how life develops for everyone. And yet, though we all face the same kinds of questions, wrestle with the same attempts to avoid them—in the end we all face a series of trials, of tests, of triumphs.

The truth is that we each play the music of our lives in distinct and distinguishing ways. We can learn by listening to others, of course, but, in the end, it's not about the overarching melody of life so much; it's not about someone else's answers. No, it's really more about the way we ourselves choose to play every single chord of it that will determine the sounds we leave behind for others to hear as they go.

As this book implies, for me those choices have returned again and again to three areas: the nature and place of God in life, the meaning of spirituality in a secular culture and the demand to understand what it means to be a woman. In a man's world, in a man's definitions, in a man's church.

If truth were told, God has forever been a factor in my life. This was the God who "took my daddy to heaven," my mother told me at his coffin, "because he had been such a good daddy." This was a God to keep your eye on. And "God's friends"—two nuns who had taught him in school—were there, she went on, "to give his soul to God." So nuns began to fascinate me, too. Indeed, God was a theme that dogged me everywhere.

My mother was not an avid churchgoer, but she was devout, clear about her values, and equally clear about things she thought made no sense. Learning all of that at the age of three, some would argue, is a heavy burden for a child. For me it was a rudder, an end point in times of fear and pain. It was an invitation to think, to pursue ideas, to "examine before buying" anything.

It was a point in the universe where things pointed true north for a change.

As a result, perhaps, the contrariness of the theology of God that someone apparently wanted me to accept—that God gave us free will but punished us for using it, for instance—agitated my soul, weakened my belief, before anyone expected me to have any. God, the gift-giver, who denied me important gifts and wanted me to "give them up," was a problem, too.

Indeed, it was the Cosmic God to whom I turned, young but thoughtful, that saved me in the end. It was this God that showed me that the gifts I'd been given was the life I was meant to live. It was in the arena of "believe but be prepared to be uncertain" that gave me a sense of the God who dwelt within me, not outside me, like a prize I was supposed to earn.

It's out of that nagging question of life that spirituality, not theology, took hold of my soul. In a Benedictine monastery whose foundation is embedded in the psalms, the gospels, sacred reading and communal service to the world around us, religion become a part of life. Spirituality became the call to find the God of creation everywhere and so accept the notion of being co-creators ourselves.

Finally, the woman's question agitated my entire life. Why a family uncle did not help his wife to carry their three small children—even with "one on the way"—my mother told me, was because "men said it was 'unmanly' for a man to carry babies." That was enough to put paid to sexism for me. I was an only child who had been taught that I could do anything a boy could do, at least until he became a man. This was a new song, I knew, that needed to be sung. Loudly. For all our sakes.

Those chords—the presence of God, the call to spiritual insight, and the rejection of sexism—have carried me through life. I have run into walls, not bridges, to those ideas everywhere, yes, but there has also been a drumbeat of truth under all of it.

In the face of every obstacle, I heard the call of God to wake up, to speak out, to leave some melodies behind. Then, perhaps others could sing new songs of the truth within them, too, so that generations to come might also wake up.

If we awaken. Now.

Sources

Chapter 1. "Theology of Domination" from *Women's Studies Encyclopedia* vol. III, ed. Helen Tierney (New York: Greenwood Press, 1991). Used with permission of ABC-CLIO, LLC.

Chapter 2. "Women in the Church: A New Pentecost in Process" from *The Papacy and the People of God*, ed. Gary MacEoin (Maryknoll, NY: Orbis Books, 1997). Used with permission.

Chapter 3. "Discipleship: The Questionable Measure of Christianity" from *Light Burdens, Heavy Blessings: Challenges of Church and Culture in the Post Vatican II Era*, ed. Mary Heather MacKinnon, Moni McIntyre, and Mary Ellen Sheehan (Cincinnati: Franciscan Press, 2000). Used with permission of the Sisters of the Immaculate Heart of Mary, Monroe, MI.

Chapter 4. "Wanted: The Other Half of the Church" from *Unfinished Journey: the Church 40 Years after Vatican II*, ed. Austin Ivereigh (New York: Continuum Publishing, 2003). Used with permission of Bloomsbury Publishing Plc.

Chapter 5. "Mary" by Joan Chittister, OSB, excerpted from *Awake My Soul: Contemporary Catholics on Traditional Devotions*, ed. James Martin, SJ. Copyright © 2004 by James Martin, SJ, published by Loyola Press. Used by permission of Loyola Press. Visit *www.LoyolaPress.com* for more information.

Chapter 6. "The Visitation" from *Holiness and the Feminine Spirit: The Art of Janet McKenzie*, ed. Susan Perry (Maryknoll, NY: Orbis Books, 2009). Used with permission.

Chapter 7. "God Our Father; God Our Mother: In Search of the Divine Feminine" from *Women, Spirituality, and Transformative Leadership*, ed. Kathe Schaaf, Kay Lindahl, et al. (Nashville: Skylight Paths, 2011). Used with permission of Turner Publishing.

Chapter 8. "The Woman Who Wouldn't: When Vision Gives Voice to Dissent" by Joan Chittister, OSB (Copyright © 2013 by Joan D. Chittister) from *Not Less Than Everything*, ed. Catherine Wolff. Copyright © 2013 by Catherine Wolff. Used by permission of HarperCollins Publishers.

Chapter 9. "The Burden of Nonviolence" from *A New Moment: An Invitation to Nonviolence*, 1986, Pax Christi USA. Originally, "The Heaviest Burden Is No Burden." Copyright © 1986 by Joan D. Chittister.

Chapter 10. "The Place of Prophecy in Dark Times: The Light That Does Not Dim." A tribute to Rosemary Haughton, 1997. Unpublished. Copyright © 1997 by Joan D. Chittister.

Chapter 11. "Oh, Wonder of Wonders" from *How Can I Find God?* ed. James Martin, SJ (Liguori, MO: Triumph Books, 1997, rev. 2004). Used with permission from Liguori/Triumph Publications.

Chapter 12. "What Does It Mean to Be Human?" published as "Sister Joan Chittister" in *What Does It Mean to Be Human*? ed. Frederick Franck (New York: Circumstantial Publishing, 1998). Used with permission of St. Martin's Press of Macmillan Publishers.

Chapter 13. "Thirst for Beauty, Thirst for Soul" from *Creation out of Clay: The Ceramic Art and Writings of Brother Thomas* (Grand Rapids, MI: Eerdmans Publishing, 1999). Reprinted with permission of the publisher.

Chapter 14. "God Become Infinitely Larger" from *God at 2000,* ed. Marcus Borg and Ross MacKenzie (Harrisburg, PA: Morehouse Publishing, 2000). Used with permission of the Episcopal Shoppe.

Chapter 15. "Dear Sisters and Brothers of South America" from *Global Latin American Agenda*, ed. José María Vigil and Pedro Casaldáliga, Social Justice Committee, 2005. Used with permission of the Social Justice Connection, Montreal.

Chapter 16. "The Struggle between Confusion and Expectation: The Legacy of Vatican II" from *Vatican II: 50 Personal Stories*, ed. William Madges and Michael Daley (Maryknoll, NY: Orbis Books, 2012). Used with permission.

Chapter 17. "Fasting" from *Catholic Spiritual Practices,* ed. Colleen Griffith and Thomas Groome (Orleans, MA: Paraclete Press, 2012). Used with permission.

Chapter 18. "Seeds of a New Humanity" from *Sacred Seed*, 2014, The Golden Sufi Center. Used with permission, www.goldensufi.org.

Chapter 19. "Stages in the Spiritual Life" is the Foreword to *Sick, and You Cared for Me: Homilies and Reflections for Cycle B*, ed. Jim Knipper (Marco Island, FL: Clear View Publishing, 2014). Used with permission.

Chapter 20. "St. Benedict of Nursia, Benedictine Monasticism and Peace" from *World Encyclopedia of Peace*, ed. E. Laszlo, Jung Youl Yoo, and Linus Pauling (New York: Pergamon Press, 1986). Used with permission of Elsevier Limited.

Chapter 21. "Vows" from *The New Dictionary of Catholic Spirituality*, ed. Michael Downey (Collegeville, MN: Liturgical Press, 1993), Used with permission.

Chapter 22. "Old Vision for a New Age" from *A Monastic Vision for the 21st Century*, ed. Patrick Hart, OSCO (Kalamazoo, MI: Cistercian Publications, 2006). Order of Saint Benedict, Collegeville, MN. Used with permission.

Chapter 23. "The Monastic Spirit and the Pursuit of Everlasting Beauty" from *The Journey and Gift: The Ceramic Art of Brother Thomas* (Boston: Pucker Art Publications, 2006). Used with permission.

Chapter 24. "Monasticism in a Mobile World" from *Monasticism Today*, 2018, Buckfast Abbey, Devon, England. Used with permission.

Chapter 25. "Being Benedictine 'To Be or Not to Be: That Is the Question'" is a major address given at the online conference, Being Benedictine, in May 2021. Copyright © by Joan D. Chittister.

Some chapters have been slightly adapted for this volume.